Éirí amach Na Cásca 1916
The Easter Rising of 1916.

Outline of the events which occurred during the Easter Rising of 1916: illustrated with photographs from the books, 'The Dublin Rebellion' and 'Dublin After the Six days Insurrection'.

2016 marks the centennial year of the 1916 Easter Rising. Staged over six days during Easter week 1916, the Rising is believed to be the most significant event in modern Ireland's history as it paved the way for the Irish War of Independence (1919-1921) and the subsequent Irish Civil War (1922-1923).

The Rising, which began on Easter Monday the 24th April, was fought by the Irish Volunteers Force (IVF) and the Irish Citizen Army (ICA) but it was masterminded by members of the Irish Republican Brotherhood's (IRB's) Secret Military Council. Lead by Thomas Clarke and Séan MacDermott, the council was also comprised of Eamonn Ceannt, James Connolly, Thomas MacDonagh, Patrick Pearse and Joseph Plunkett.

The leaders envisaged the Rising as a historical event which would mark the end of British rule in Ireland and the creation of a new Irish Republic. They outlined their aims and ambitions for the rebellion in a document entitled the *Proclamation of the Republic*.

Easter Monday, 24th of April 1916:

Originally the Rising had been planned to begin on Easter Sunday. The leader of the IVF, Eoin MacNeill had cancelled the plans when he had learned that the weapons needed by the Volunteers to fight had not landed in Kerry on Good Friday. However, the members of the IRB secret council decided to defy his command and issued orders that the Rising would now go ahead on Easter Monday. As a result at 11am on Easter Monday, approximately 400 Volunteers and ICA members intent on participating in the insurrection gathered outside Liberty Hall. After midday the troops marched to their various garrisons. James Connolly accompanied by Patrick Pearse and Joseph Plunkett led his 150 strong force to the General Post Office (GPO) situated on Upper Sackville Street. Commandant Michael Mallin marched his rank and file to St. Stephen's Green. The other Volunteer battalions led by Edward 'Ned' Daly, Thomas MacDonagh, Eamon de Valera and Éamonn Ceannt had already gathered their Volunteers closer to the locations which they intended to occupy. Daly and his troops occupied the Four Courts and surrounding areas in the North West of the city. Thomas MacDonagh's troops seized Jacob's Biscuit Factory while Eamon de Valera's 130 men (he wouldn't allow any women to fight in his garrison) occupied principally Boland's Mill Bakery and a number of surrounding buildings to cover Beggars Bush Barracks and the main road and railway from Kingstown Harbour, (now known as Dún Laoghaire). Éamonn Ceannt commanded approximately 100 men who occupied the South Dublin Union as well as establishing outposts in Jameson's Distillery in Marrowbone Lane, Watkin's Brewery in Ardee Street and Roe's Distillery in James Street.

North Earl Street, from Lower Sackville Street

Henry Street, Showing the north side of the GPO

The headquarters of the military council for most of Easter week was the GPO and it was here that five of the members of the IRB's military council chose to remain positioned from Monday until Friday. They were Pearse, Connolly, Plunkett, Séan MacDermott and Thomas Clarke.

At the same time as the Volunteers were preparing to march to their garrisons, a raid was attempted by the Volunteers on the British army's Magazine Fort in Phoenix Park. Hopes to start the Rising with the sucessful seizure of British arms and ammunition, as well as blowing up the fort, were dashed when the attack fell apart after the pointless murder of the 14 year old son of the fort's commandant. Though the explosion went off, it was not loud enough to be heard in the city. Meanwhile, Sean Connolly and his 30 ICA rebels were unable to seize Dublin Castle although they did shoot dead a police sentry and gain access to the guardroom where they overpowered the British soldiers present.

Tuesday 25th to Saturday 29th of April 1916:

The British authorities recovered quickly from their initial surprise at the outbreak of the Rising. The failure of the Volunteers to seize control of Dublin's communications (including the telegraph and the railways) meant contact between the authorities in Dublin and London was maintained. By Monday evening the Lord Lieutenant of Ireland, Lord Wimbourne had called for military reinforcements from England and during Monday night the Officer's Training Corps at Trinity College was reinforced by 1,600 troops transported in via railway from their Curragh Barracks. On Tuesday morning Wimbourne decided to declare Martial Law in Dublin and handed civil power over to General William Lowe. Uncertain of just how many rebels there actually were, Lowe focused on 'the establishment of a central axis of communiction running from Kingsbridge to the North Wall and Trinity College, followed by the cordoning off of the main rebel positions'.

By Wednesday, Martial Law had been enforced across Ireland and British reinforcements were landing at Dublin Port and Kingstown Port as well as being drafted in from their Irish garrisons in Belfast and the Curragh. Eventually, by the end of the Rising, approximately 16,000 British troops would be in Dublin. Their arms and ammunitions, including four eighteen-punder field guns, vastly outnumbered the Volunteers supplies and the arrival of the British vessel, the *Helga* on Wednesday morning exacerbated the situation. At 8am the *Helga* started shelling Liberty Hall, chosen for symbolic reasons because it was where the Volunteers had assembled. Then the army started firing on the other Volunteer garrisons, espicially the GPO and Boland's Mill and a battle raged

Loyal Volunteers on duty at GPO - military passing

at Mount Street Bridge throughout the day. Overnight troops had continued to arrive from Britain to reinforce the British military position. Upon disembarking at Kingstown, these troops recieved a warm welcome from the locals and set off immediately to march towards the city. Around the Grand Canal, heavy fighting broke out as the Volunteers tried to prevent the troops advancing into the city. Strategically hidden in the town buildings on either side of Mount Street, the Volunteers opened fire on the soldiers as they marched past, resulting in the wounding and deaths of over 200 soldiers. Wednesday afternoon also witnessed the first surrender of significance when the Volunteers posted at Mendicity Institute decided to surrrender after coming under machine gun and rifle fire. Later it would become common knowledge that three innocent men, two journalists Thomas Dickson and Patrick MacIntyre and the well-known pacifist Francis Sheehy Skeffington, were executed on Wednesday morning by firing squad in Portobello Barracks. Their executions had been ordered by Captain J.C. Bowen-Colthurst, later to be certified medically insane, because he was convinced that they were involved in the Rising.

On Thursday, the principal Volunteer garrisons, namely the GPO, the Four Courts, Jacob's Factory and Boland's Mill continued to experience heavy bombardment. After the Mount Street massacre, the British had decided that it was better to fire on the garrisons instead of trying to charge in and having to engage the rebels in physical combat. This decision was reinforced after attempts to attack a rebel garrison on North King Street, (behind the main Four Courts garrison), left 11 soldiers dead and 28 wounded as the South Staffordshire Regiment advanced only 150 yards down the street. As well as the deaths of 15 civilians after the South Staffordshire Regiment conducted systematic searches of homes along the street.The shelling intensified and the leaders of the Rising became convinced that they would soon be overcome. Many of the smaller rebel outposts withdrew back to the relative safety of the larger Volunteer garrisons while some Volunteers decided to abandon official outposts entirely and took to occupying rooms in ordinary civilian homes and buildings. Those under the command of Michael Mallin in St Stephen's Green abandoned their freshly-dug trenches and retreated to the nearby Royal College of Suregons building where they remained until surrender. At the GPO James Connolly was shot as he organised fresh outspost around the GPO in an attempt to prolong the Volunteers' defence of their headquarters.

Overnight the British continued to shell the GPO and Sackville street. In the GPO, the Volunteers watched as the opposite side of the street, including Clerys were engulfed in a firestorm which caused the glass in the windows to melt. The heat of the fire was so great that it caused the mail bags within the GPO to burst into flames, despite the Volunteer's best efforts to keep cooling the building by hosing it down with water.

The Surrender:

The decision was made to evacuate the burning GPO on Friday afternoon. The retreat proved deadly for many, including The O'Rahilly who led the charge down Moore Street towards the British barricade. 700 Volunteers sought refuge in Moore Street's tenement houses and they spent the night trying to burrow their way through the houses towards Sackville Lane. In their efforts to break down interior walls, the Volunteers frequently ended up killing and injuring many of the civilan inhabitants of the houses.

Clarke, Connolly, MacDermott, Pearse and Plunkett successfully made their way to 16 Moore Street where they spent the night sleeping on the living room furniture. On Saturday 29th April, a meeting was convened around the bed in the backroom where Connolly lay injured. The decision was made to surrender and Elizabeth O'Farrell was dispatched to meet with General Lowe and express the Irish Republican Army's desire to agree terms of surrender. By 3.30pm Pearse (accompanied by Nurse O'Farrell) officially surrendered to General Lowe at the top of Moore Street. An order was issued by Pearse and countersigned by Connolly that all Volunteers were to surrender. The document read:

In order to prevent the further slaughter of Dublin Citizens, and in the hope of saving the lives of our followers now surrendered and hopelessly outnumbered, the members of the Provisional Government present at headquarters have agreed to an unconditional surrender, and the commandants of the various districts in the City and County will order their commands to lay down arms.

Nurse O'Farrell delivered the order to all the garrisons but sporadic fighting continued until Sunday. By then General John Maxwell, the new British commander- in-chief had taken over military control from General Lowe.

Rounding Up The Rebels - A Sinn Fein Prisoner Being Conveyed To The Castle

The GPO:

The GPO was the only garrison of the Volunteers to be wholly destroyed during the course of the Rising. By Saturday 29th, all that remained of the building was the facade. The building would not be restored to it's former glory until the 1920s when the Cumann na nGaedheal government took on the task of rebuilding it. In the meantime, the GPO staff opened a temporary office beside the Rotunda Hospital at the top of Sackville Street (now O'Connell Street). Today, as well as operating as a functioning post office, the building houses a museum dedicated to the history of An Post and exhibits an original copy of The Proclamation of the Irish Republic. One of which had been pinned to the pillars outside the GPO's main entrance on Easter Monday after Pearse had read it aloud to the assembled crowd comprised of enthusiastic Volunteers and curious Dublin onlookers.

POBLACHT NA H EIREANN.

THE PROVISIONAL GOVERNMENT OF THE IRISH REPUBLIC TO THE PEOPLE OF IRELAND.

IRISHMEN AND IRISHWOMEN: In the name of God and of the dead generations from which she receives her old tradition of nationhood, Ireland, through us, summons her children to her flag and strikes for her freedom.

Having organised and trained her manhood through her secret revolutionary organisation, the Irish Republican Brotherhood, and through her open military organisations, the Irish Volunteers and the Irish Citizen Army, having patiently perfected her discipline, having resolutely waited for the right moment to reveal itself, she now seizes that moment, and, supported by her exiled children in America and by gallant allies in Europe, but relying in the first on her own strength, she strikes in full confidence of victory.

We declare the right of the people of Ireland to the ownership of Ireland, and to the unfettered control of Irish destinies, to be sovereign and indefeasible. The long usurpation of that right by a foreign people and government has not extinguished the right, nor can it ever be extinguished except by the destruction of the Irish people. In every generation the Irish people have asserted their right to national freedom and sovereignty; six times during the past three hundred years they have asserted it in arms. Standing on that fundamental right and again asserting it in arms in the face of the world, we hereby proclaim the Irish Republic as a Sovereign Independent State, and we pledge our lives and the lives of our comrades-in-arms to the cause of its freedom, of its welfare, and of its exaltation among the nations.

The Irish Republic is entitled to, and hereby claims, the allegiance of every Irishman and Irishwoman. The Republic guarantees religious and civil liberty, equal rights and equal opportunities to all its citizens, and declares its resolve to pursue the happiness and prosperity of the whole nation and of all its parts, cherishing all the children of the nation equally, and oblivious of the differences carefully fostered by an alien government, which have divided a minority from the majority in the past.

Until our arms have brought the opportune moment for the establishment of a permanent National Government, representative of the whole people of Ireland and elected by the suffrages of all her men and women, the Provisional Government, hereby constituted, will administer the civil and military affairs of the Republic in trust for the people.

We place the cause of the Irish Republic under the protection of the Most High God, Whose blessing we invoke upon our arms, and we pray that no one who serves that cause will dishonour it by cowardice, inhumanity, or rapine. In this supreme hour the Irish nation must, by its valour and discipline and by the readiness of its children to sacrifice themselves for the common good, prove itself worthy of the august destiny to which it is called.

Signed on Behalf of the Provisional Government,

THOMAS J. CLARKE,

SEAN Mac DIARMADA, THOMAS MacDONAGH,

P. H. PEARSE, EAMONN CEANNT,

JAMES CONNOLLY. JOSEPH PLUNKETT.

Picture Number 6:

Easter Monday, 24th of April 1916:

Owing to the bank holiday, the GPO had only been operating on Easter Monday morning with a reduced staff. As the post office was only offering a few essential services, only a few members of the public were using it.

When the Volunteers entered the building in the early afternoon of Easter Monday, they immediately ordered the staff and public to leave. Realising that the rebels were intending to cut the GPO's telegraph communication network with Dublin Castle and London, the 20 GPO telegraph staff, alongside some unarmed British soldiers employed to guard the GPO, barricaded their office doors and refused to comply.

The staff were eventually forced to leave and the soldiers taken prisoner by the Volunteers. However, recognising the essential role communications would play in the coming days, the 20 GPO staff simply moved to the Crown Alley telephone exchange, where they remained until the end of the Rising, passing on urgent messages between the British and Irish authorities. GPO engineers also worked tirelessly over the course of Easter Week to repair the telegraph lines cut by the Volunteers.

Smouldering Ruins:

More than 200 buildings were damaged over the course of Easter week. Estimates of the cost of destruction sustained by Dublin as a direct result of the Rising usually suggest the figure to be over £2.5 million.

However, no price can be put on the number of lives lost and the injuries sustained by both civilians, soldiers and the Volunteers. In total 450 people were killed, 2,614 injured and 9 declared missing during the Rising. The numbers would have been higher except for the hard work of Dublin's emergency services, such as the Fire Brigade and the ambulances.

Dublin's hospitals remained open throughout the Rising and did their best to tend the wounded in trying conditions as there was no gas or electricity and operations had to be conducted by candlelight. By the end of the week the Mater Hospital had admitted 73 people, another 600 were treated in Jervis Street Hospital and Richmond Hospital treated another 300.

Local undertakers did their best to collect the dead from the city's hospitals and morgues as well as from the streets and destroyed buildings across the city. The unseasonably warm weather meant it was urgent that the dead and decomposing bodies were buried quickly so as to prevent the spread of disease and infection. Consequently many of the dead were buried in unmarked graves in gardens, yards and even Dublin Castle.

Many animals had also been killed during the fighting as they strayed into the line of fire - or were killed to be eaten by the starving Volunteers and Dublin civilians - their remains also had to be buried in mass graves.

Due to the urgency in disposing of the dead, few records were kept and therefore in the years that followed it proved impossible for some families to locate the graves of their dead.

The Rebel Leaders: Pádraig Pearse:

Picture Number 7a:

Patrick Pearse

Patrick Henry Pearse was born on the 10th November 1879, at 27 Great Brunswick Street (now known as Pearse Street). As the eldest son of an English stonemason, James Pearse, who had emigrated to Ireland in the 1860s. Pearse enjoyed a middle-class upbringing alongside his siblings Margaret, William ('Willie') and Mary Brigid. His parents had placed great emphasis on their sons education and the two boys were enrolled in the Christian Brothers School located on Westland Row. Unlike his younger brother Willie, Patrick did very well in CBS and he continued his academic studies at the Royal University of Ireland. He graduated with a BA in modern languages and enrolled to become a barrister at the King's Inn. He was called to the Bar in June 1901.

Pearse was ambivalent about pursuing a career in law. Believing that the key to the future of the Irish language lay in education, he opened his own school in 1908 and named it St. Enda after the patron saint of the Aran Islands. Initially located in Cullenswood House, Oakly Road, the school moved to Rathfarnham in 1910. St. Ita's school for girls, the 'sister' school of St Enda's took over the Cullenswood address in 1910. Eager to promote bilingual education in English and Irish, Pearse was aided in his endeavour by Thomas MacDonagh who acted as the assistant headmaster.

Having fostered a love of Irish during his childhood thanks to his grandaunt Margaret's stories on Wolfe Tone, Robert Emmet and the Fenians and the enthusiasm of his teachers in CBS to teach Irish, Pearse had joined the Gaelic League as a teenager and rapidly rose through the ranks of the organisation to join the Executive Committee in 1898. His close friendship with MacDonagh brought him into contact with many Irish nationalist dramatists including William Butler Yeats.

The IRB and the Volunteers:

Invited to give a speech at the IRB's commemorative gathering in March 1911 for Robert Emmet, Pearse's skills as an orator impressed Tom Clarke and Sean MacDermott, who realised how useful he could be to the IRB. Having continued to demonstrate his abilities throughout 1912 as he spoke in favour of the Irish Home Rule Bill and gave an emotional speech at a commemorative event for Wolfe Tone in early 1913, Pearse was sworn into the IRB by Bulmer Hobson in December 1913. The IRB was a secret organisation dedicated to overthrowing British rule in Ireland through the use of 'physical force'. To achieve this, they had decided to form an independent Irish nationalist militia in November 1913, inspired by the Ulster Volunteer Force (UVF) which had been formed in 1913. The Irish Volunteer Force (IVF) was founded in November 1913, and from the IVF's inception Pearse played a prominent role. Following the split in the IVF after the outbreak of the First World War as prominent nationalist politician John Redmond, encouraged members of the IVF to join the British army much to the dismay of Eoin MacNeill (the founder of the IVF), Pearse and a number of the other IRB men involved in the IVF began plotting to defy any attempt made by the British to impose conscription in Ireland. Pearse was appointed director of military organisation and oversaw the creation of military structures within the IVF.

On 1st August 1915, Pearse delivered the tribute at the graveside of the famous Fenian, Jerimiah O'Donovan Rossa. The funeral brought together the ICA, the IRB and the Volunteers. In his speech which Clarke had insisted must be 'as hot as hell', Pearse spoke of blood sacrafice. It was an idea that proved popular among many members of the congregation and plans developed to stage an insurrection against the British. The grounds of St. Enda's became an important centre for drilling and training the Volunteers. It was also the perfect meeting place for the members of the IRB's secret military council. Unsurprisingly, many of Pearse's students in St. Enda's participated in the Rising, including the P.E. teacher Con Colbert. These boys had been members of Fianna Éireann, the Irish equivalent of the Boy Scouts, founded by Bulmer Hobson and Countess Markievicz in 1909.

Pearse was the figurehead of the Rising and as commander-in-chief and president of the new Republic, it was his duty on Easter Monday to read aloud the Proclamation of the Irish Republic on the steps of the GPO. Following a court martial trial, he was found guilty of leading the Rising and was executed by firing squad on 3rd May 1916, in Kilmainham Gaol. Aged just 36 years old, he was buried in Arbour Hill Cemetery.

James Connolly:

Picture Number 7b:

James Connolly

James Connolly, the youngest son of John and Mary Connolly, was born in the Edinburgh tenement lodgings 107 Cowgate on 5th June 1868. The site of the tenement (now the location of Herriot Watt University), was situated in St. Patrick's Parish, a densely-populated parish in which the 14,000 Irish immigrants lived in such poverty that disease was rampant and the area was known locally as 'Little Ireland'. As his father was employed by the local corporation as a manure carter, James grew up in relative poverty. His schooling was limited as he started working at the age of 9 in order to help keep the family above the bread-line. James enlisted (under a false name) to the British army when he was 14 years of age. Serving as a private in the First Battalion of the King's Liverpool Regiment, James was stationed in various Irish barracks from 1882-1889, including Castlebar, Cork and Dublin. It was in Dublin that Connolly met his wife, Lille Reynolds when the two missed a tram at Merrion Square, which failed to stop. Having deserted the army in late 1888/1889 as his regiment prepared to leave for India, the couple decided to emigrate and marry in Perth in April 1890. Their marriage proved successful and they had seven children: Mona, Nora, Aideen, Ina, Maria, Roderic 'Roddy' and Fiona.

Settling in his hometown of Edinburgh, James became involved in labour politics as a result of his brother John's close relationship with John Leslie, a prominent member of the Social Democratic Federation. Soon he was writing articles and reports for various Socialist publications including *Justice*. In need of work, Connolly and his family moved to Dublin in 1896 when the Dublin Socialist Club invited him to become their paid organiser on a weekly salary of £1. Here he founded the Irish Socialist Republican Party (IRSP) and produced a manifesto for the party which spoke of a desire to attain 'universal suffrage' and the establishment of an Irish republic- themes that would later be central in the *Proclamation of the Irish Republic*. In 1898 believing that social revolution started by the Irish lower classes was required to improve living standards, Connolly launched a newspaper the *Worker's Republic*.

Financial difficulties forced him to emigrate to relatives who lived in Troy, New York state in 1903. There he and his family remained until 1910 when he returned to Ireland. While in the United States,

Connolly was employed in various occupations including as an insuranceman and a mechanical operator for the Singer Sewing Machine Factory.

It was not until his return from working in America in 1910 that Connolly became convinced of the significant role that Irish nationalism could play in helping attain the republic he desired. As a national organiser for the Socialist Party of Ireland, he published various pamphlets which insisted that the Irish working class needed to 'organise itself industrially and politically with the end in view of gaining control and mastery of the entire resources of the country'. Financial pressure again forced the Connolly family to move to Belfast where Connolly became involved in the Irish Transport and General Worker's Union (ITGWU). Following his successful organisation of the Belfast docker's strike in the summer of 1911, he was elected in Janauy 1912 to the Dublin Corporation. In August 1913, he was summoned to Dublin to help assist James Larkin with the organisation of the Dublin Lockout.

Connolly and the Irish Volunteers

Though the Lockout ultimately proved unsuccesful, it acted as the catalyst that brought about the foundation of the ITGWU's own civilian militia- the Irish Citizen Army (ICA). The ICA was founded on the 23rd November 1913, two days prior to the IVF's foundation. Captain Jack White oversaw regular drilling of the ICA and by 1914 though the Lockout had ended, membership continued to grow. On replacing Larkin in Dublin's ITGWU, after Larkin moved to the United States, Connolly attempted to afilliate the ICA with the Volunteers. However, the leadership of the Volunteers were wary of Connolly's hot temper and extreme ambitions. Only when it became obvious to his friends Tom Clarke, Séan MacDermott and Countess Markievicz that Connolly intended to stage a rebellion with the ICA regardless of the IVF, did the IRB's secret military council agree to tell Connolly of their plans for a Rising.

Connolly agreed to the plans and took an active role in the final preparations, conducting reconaissance missions around Dublin Bay with Dr. Kathleen Lynn, in an attempt to locate where the Germans should land. When the Rising began, he was effectively the Commander-in-chief as he had been elected Vice-President of the Provisional Government and also acted as leader of the entire ICA fraction. Having been shot in the arm while setting up new outposts around the GPO, Connolly was eventually disabled after a stray bullet shattered his ankle. He spent the rest of the Rising issuing orders from a mattress in the GPO and later had to be carried to the relative safety of 16 Moore Street.

Execution

Following a court martial trial, Connolly was sentenced to death by firing squad. Unable to stand, he was carried by stretcher to Kilmainham's courtyard and then tied to a chair before being shot. His execution on the morning of the 12th May was arguably one of the most controversial owing to his ill health. British Prime Minister Herbert Asquith, on hearing of the execution later that day when he arrived in Dublin, insisted on all other executions being cancelled.

The Four Courts: 6 days after The Insurrection

Located on Inns Quay, Dublin, the Four Courts as it is known today, were built between the years 1786 – 1796.

It served initially as the main public records of Ireland building and was originally designed by Thomas Cooley. After his death the renowned architect of the time James Gandon was appointed to finish the building as it stands today.

During the Easter Rising, The Four Courts lay witness to some of the most intense fighting which took place in Church St/ North King St/ North Brunswick area of the city, one mile to the west of Sackville Street, now known as O' Connell St. It was a strategic area as it controlled the main route between the Military barracks and the GPO.

Led by Limerick born Commandant Edward (Ned) Daly, the 1st Battalion of the Dublin Brigade, occupied the Four Courts and the adjacent streets on the north bank of the Liffey.

Daly was born on February 25th 1891 in 26 Frederick Street now known as O' Curry Street, Limerick City. He was the only son of Edward and Catherine Daly who parented ten children. He was the youngest brother of Kathleen Clarke who was married to another Rising activist Thomas Clarke. Ned's father, also a Fenian had died five months prior to his only son's birth at the age of forty one.

It is not known exactly when Edward Daly joined the Irish Republican Brotherhood; however it has been confirmed that he was a member of the newly founded Irish Volunteers of 1913. He moved quickly up the ranks and was highly regarded amongst his peers, thus becoming the youngest member to hold rank of Commandant during the Easter Rising and thus the youngest to be executed in the aftermath.

It is believed that six months prior to the Rising Daly had sought employment in Shorthall's Building Contractors. This company was engaged in carrying out works on the complex allowing Daly to gain detailed knowledge of the layout of the Fort and the garrison's roster. The task of First Battalion was to signal the start of the rebellion through an explosion at the Magazine Fort in the Phoenix Park.

In order to move closer to the Magazine Fort without arousing suspicion the volunteers began a football match near the complex.

While Ned Daly's battalion normally numbered 400, only 150 turned out on the day, but the numbers grew over the following days as word of the Rising spread. The Headquarters were at the entrance to the North Dublin Union (later St Laurence's Hospital) on North Brunswick Street.

The first skirmish occurring on Monday afternoon when Volunteers in the Four Courts got the better of a party of Lancers

Four Courts
Na Ceithre Cúirteanna

Picture Number 2:

This Photograph taken by T.W Murphy, of the Four Courts after the Insurrection illustrates the damage caused, mainly consisting of broken glass caused by rifle firing.

(cavalry) escorting lorries loaded with munitions. On Wednesday the Volunteers captured two enemy positions in the area, the Bridewell which was held by police and Linenhall Barracks, which was occupied by unarmed army clerks.

By Thursday the 27th of April the area was effectively cordoned off by the South Staffordshire and Sherwood Forest regiments. The fighting continued until Saturday evening the 29th of April when the news of Pearse's surrender filtered through. Commandant Daly is said to have shown great concern for the civilian community; he took over Monks' Bakery and arranged for the distribution of bread to the local community. Ireland's main courts complex, the Four Courts survived the Rising, but was destroyed during the Civil War in 1922. It was rebuilt and reopened in 1932.

St. Stephen's Green and the Royal College of Surgeons During the Easter Rising:

Born in Dublin on December 1st 1874, Commandant Michael Mallin second in command of the Easter Rising under James Connolly and in turn his second in command, Countess Markievicz, were assigned to St Stephen's Green, a rectangular park, approximately twenty acres in size located a mile south of the General Post Office and close to Jacob's biscuit factory.

The current membership of the Irish Citizen Army (ICA) was approximately 400; it is estimated that 200-250 turned out during the Rising, most of them serving with Mallin in the St Stephen's Green area, the main exceptions being those with Seán Connolly at City Hall.

Mallin proceeded to fortify his position, posting men in some of the houses overlooking the Green and setting men to work digging trenches to cover the entrances. He dispatched parties to take

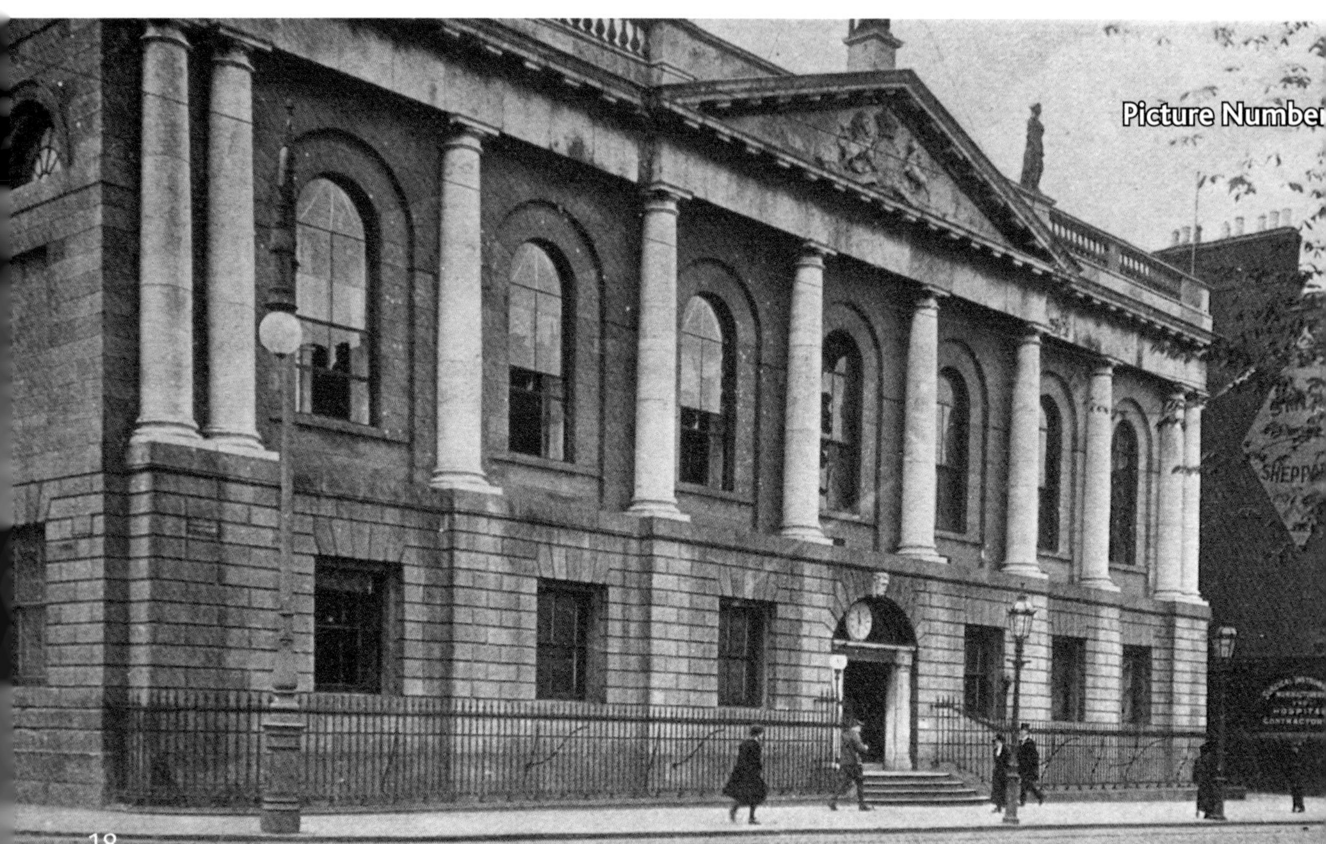

ROYAL COLLEGE OF SURGEONS WHERE COUNTESS MARKIEVICZ SURRENDERED, DU

over Harcourt Street railway station, J. & T. Davy's (now Portobello) public house at the junction of South Richmond Street, Charlemont Mall and houses at Leeson Street Bridge. It soon transpired that St Stephen's Green was a vulnerable position, as it was overlooked by the Shelbourne Hotel and some other tall buildings that had not been occupied by Mallin's forces.

Mallin had military experience, having served for fourteen years in the British army, part of the time as a non-commissioned officer (NCO). Presumably, when St Stephen's Green was originally selected as a position it was expected that there would be enough men to occupy the Shelbourne Hotel and all the other tall buildings, but that was not the case. The British directed machine gun fire from the Shelbourne onto the Green late on Monday, as a result of which Mallin abandoned most of it by Tuesday.

The majority of the ICA forces then garrisoned the Royal College of Surgeons immediately to the west of the Green. As General Lowe concentrated on the GPO and the Four Courts, the College of Surgeons garrison was involved in little action until the order for surrender came the following Sunday.

Mallin surrendered on Sunday, 30th April 1916 when ordered to do so by Connolly. At his trial by court-martial he downplayed his involvement. In his statement, Mallin said, "I had no commission whatever in the Citizen Army. I was never taken into the confidence of James Connolly. I was under the impression that we were going out for manoeuvres on Sunday." He added, "Shortly after my arrival at St Stephen's Green the firing started and Countess Markievicz ordered me to take command of the men as I had been so long associated with them. I felt I could not leave them and from that time I joined the rebellion."

Convicted by a court martial presided over by Colonal EWSK Maconchy, Mallin was executed by firing squad on the 8th May 1916. The presiding officer at his court martial was Colonel EWSK Maconchy. In his last letter to his wife, who was pregnant with their fifth child, Mallin stated that "I find no fault with the soldiers or the police" and admonished her "to pray for all the souls who fell in this fight, Irish and English." He commented "so must Irishmen pay for trying to make Ireland a free nation." He wrote to his baby son, "Joseph, my little man, be a priest if you can", and also requested that his daughter Una become a nun, which she did.

Dún Laoghaire Mallin DART station is named after Michael Mallin.

Countess Constance Markievicz: *(née Gore-Booth)*

Countess Constance Markievicz

The eldest of three daughters and two sons, Constance Georgina Gore-Booth was born on the 4th February 1868 at Buckingham Gate in London to Sir Henry Gore-Booth and Georgina Mary Gore-Booth. Descended from 17th century English planters, the Gore-Booths had settled at Lissadell House situated in north county Sligo. Owing to her father's career as an explorer, Constance regularly travelled abroad during her childhood. Sir Henry Gore-Booth was also a philanthropist and his generosity towards his tenants had a significant impact on both Constance and her four siblings, especially her sister Eva. The children's upbring reflected their social standing and Constance was educated at home by a governess. In her childhood she gained an appreciation for the arts, undoubtedly influenced by the family's close relationship with W.B. Yeats.

Choosing to pursue a career in the arts, Constance studied at the Slade School of Art in London, where she was also introduced to politics thanks to her involvement in the National Union of Woman's Suffrage Societies (NUWSS). She would later move to Paris to continue her studies, but she maintained an interest in womens suffrage within Ireland and presided over a meeting of the Sligo Women's Suffrage Society in 1896. While in Paris, she met the Polish Count Casimir Dunin-Markievicz, a fellow art student. Marrying in London in 1900, the couple's daughter Maeve was born in 1901. Leaving her with Constance's mother, the young couple returned to Paris for another year before returning and settling in Dublin. Though Maeve would spend most of her childhood residing in Sligo at Lissadell with her grandparents from 1908 onwards.

Countess Constance Markievicz

The couple's shared desire to become involved in Dublin's cultural circles through hosting their own art exhibitions and producing and acting in plays at the Abbey Theatre could not prevent their marriage breaking down in 1909. Keeping her married name, Markievicz joined Arthur Griffith's political party Sinn Féin and the feminist organisation Inghinidhe na hÉireann (Daughters of Ireland). Though her main political aspirations were still tied to women's suffrage, by 1909 she had become increasingly involved in the Irish nationalist movement. Along with leading nationalist Bulmer Hobson, Markievicz played a pivotal role in establishing the youth organisation, Fianna Éireann in 1909. In 1911 she would meet James Connolly as they prepared to risk arrest and

protest against George V's royal visit to Dublin. Both she and Connolly would remain close friends until his execution and he would always stay at her home when visiting Dublin, though his pride forced him to pay for his lodgings.

They shared a belief in the need for universal suffrage and as a result Markievicz became an enthusiastic supporter of the Women Worker's Union, when it was established in 1911. During the 1913 Dublin Lockout she would help organise and run soup kitchens in the slums of Dublin and in Liberty Hall. Her efforts would see her rewarded with the appointment as the honourary secretary of the ICA. Fiercely opposed to the outbreak of the First World War, she co-founded the Irish Neutrality League in 1914 and supported the small minority of Volunteers who refused to follow Redmond's instruction to participate in the war. Having played a key role in the merging of Inghinidhe na hÉireann with Cumman na mBan, the female republican organisation established to support the IVF, Markievicz actively participated in the military training and drills which the ICA and Fianna underwent during 1914-1916.

Like Connolly, Markievicz favoured an armed rebellion against the British authorities and she was keen to participate. Resplendent in a specially designed military uniform and brandishing a revolver, Lieutenant Markievicz was appointed to act as Chauffeur to Dr. Kathleen Lynn, the Volunteer's Chief Medical Officer. Eager to play a more active role, Markievicz would drive off to join Michael Mallin and his men in St. Stephen's Green - leaving Lynn standing on the steps of the Royal College of Surgeons.

As second in command to Mallin, Markievicz would later retreat to the College of Surgeons when the British machine gun fire from the rooftops of the buildings surrounding St. Stephens Green grew too intense. She and her fellow ICA members would remain there until they recieved Pearse and Connolly's orders to surrender. Though the British authorities offered her the option to travel by car to Dublin Castle, she refused. She was one of the only women of the 79 arrested to be placed in solitary confinement in Kilmainham.

Courtmartialled on 4th May 1916 and although found guilty of having participated in the Rising and shooting dead a British solider, her death sentence was commuted on the grounds of her sex. Markievicz was initially transferred to Mountjoy Prison and later deported to Aylesbury Prison in England, where she remained until her release in 1917, under the general amnesty signed by the British government in June 1917. In total, she served 14 months of her jail sentence.

Returning to Ireland, she converted to Catholicism and continued to play an active role in the new Sinn Féin political party. Although arrested in 1918 as part of allegedly a treacherous 'German plot', she was elected as the first female MP to the British parliament. Refusing to take her seat in London like the other Sinn Féin leaders, she returned to Dublin and was elected Minister for Labour in the first Dáil Éireann. Dying at the age of 59 on 15th July 1929 due to appendicitis complications, Markievicz remained a socialist to the end, having given away much of her wealth and spending her final days in a public hospital ward.

Liberty Hall: Halla na Saoirse

Standing on Beresford Place on Eden Quay, near the Custom House, the original Liberty Hall was a hotel before it became James Connolly's personal fortress in Dublin. During the 1913 Dublin Lock-out it served as a soup kitchen for workers' families and was run by Maud Gonne and Countess Markievicz. Following the outbreak of the First World War a banner reading "We Serve Neither King nor Kaiser, But Ireland" was hung on its front wall and Connolly's newspaper The Irish Worker was printed inside.

The newspaper was shut down by the British government for sedition under the Defence of the Realm Act (DORA). It was replaced for a short time by a paper called The Worker until that too was banned. Connolly edited a third paper, The Workers' Republic, from 1915 until the Easter Rising in 1916.

Until the Easter Rising, Liberty Hall also served as a munitions factory, where bombs and bayonets were made for the impending rebellion. It was on the street in front of the building that the leaders of the Rising assembled before their march to the General Post Office on Easter Monday. They left the building vacant throughout Easter Week, a fact unknown to the British authorities, who chose the building as the first to be shelled.

The Helga:

The TSS Helga II was not a ship of the Royal Navy; it was originally built for the Department of Agriculture in 1908 in Dublin Dockyard and was pressed into war service as an armed yacht during the First World War, serving as an anti-submarine patrol and escort vessel. Like much of the British government's response to the 1916 Rising, the Helga was rushed into service to make up for the British Army's lack of artillery.

Subsequently the Helga II gained an undeserved reputation for playing an essential part in the Rising. (Most of the damage to Dublin's city centre was caused by fire, particularly at premises like the Irish Times warehouse and Hoyt's Druggists and Oil Works, rather than by shelling.)

Liberty Hall was just three storey's high at the time and was left in rubble as illustrated in the photograph featured in the book 'The Rebellion in Dublin' when shelled by The Helga. It was the centre of pre-Rising planning with members of the IRB Military Council (Pearse, Connolly, Clarke, MacDiarmada, Ceannt and MacDonagh) meeting there to discuss the situation after the loss of the shipment of arms, Casement's arrest and MacNeill's countermand.

Most members of the Citizen Army, close to 1,000 Volunteers and members of Cumann na mBan assembled outside Liberty Hall at noon on Easter Monday the 24th of April, after removing stocks of guns, ammunition and home-made bombs and grenades stored there — before it was shelled on the Wednesday.

Liberty Hall - Head Quarters of Citizen Army, Dublin

On the 25th of April 1916 the Helga sailed from Dún Laoghaire to shell Boland's Mill, and on the following day fired from below Butt Bridge, over the loop line railway bridge at Liberty Hall.

In total the Helga fired only 40 rounds during the Rising, and it is difficult to assess the effectiveness of the fire from her guns. Indeed, two of the ship's crew refused to fire the guns during the engagement. It was completely levelled by British artillery, which fired from Tara Street, during the Rising. The Rebels found their position untenable and escaped through neighbouring houses.

Liberty Hall lay in smouldering ruins after the uprising however it was faithfully restored afterwards.

In the late 1950s Liberty Hall was declared unsafe and promptly demolished. The present building, which has sixteen storeys', was constructed between 1961 and 1965.

A 16-storey Liberty Hall was built in the 1960s. Previously home to the ITGWU and Irish Citizen Army, Liberty Hall is now the headquarters of the Services, Industrial, Professional and Technical Union (SIPTU).

The Royal Hibernian Academy:

The Royal Hibernian Academy was founded as an artist based and artist orientated institution in Ireland. It was founded on Lower Abbey Street in Dublin in 1823. It was founded as a result of almost thirty Irish artists who had petitioned the then Viceroy, Earl Talbot for a charter of incorporation allowing Irish artists to showcase their exhibitions. It flourished upon opening and by the end of the 19th century the RHA was the leading Irish Institution involved in the promotion of Irish Arts.

Wynn's Hotel & the foundation of Cumann na mBan.

Wynn's Hotel is steeped in History - built in 1845, bombed during the 1916 Rising and rebuilt in 1921 using mass concrete, the only building in Dublin to do so at this time. Miss Phoebe Wynn's, (the Proprietor at the time), was well known in the artistic and literacy circles of that time had many connections with famous figures from home and abroad which ensured that the hotel was always a hub of activity and a central meeting place for many of the characters who tread the boards of The Abbey stage.

In 1913 one of the most memorable historical events took place in the Saints & Scholars Lounge - The first meeting to establish 'The Irish Volunteer Force', chaired by Eoin Mac Neill, a Professor in UCD and attended by Padriag Pearse, The O'Rahilly, Sean MacDiarmada, and Eamonn Ceannt . The suggestion that MacNeill should take the lead in the establishment of 'The Irish Volunteer Force' is said to have been made by a Belfast Quaker, Bulmer Hobson. Hobson a political journalist working in Dublin, was the local head of the Irish Republican Brotherhood - a secret organisation whose aim was the establishment of an Irish Republic. Four of the group who attended this meeting died as a result of The 1916 Rising.

Within a few hours of the meeting being held in Wynn's, detectives from Dublin Castle called on the Manager of the Hotel to warn him not to allow further meetings of this kind - this warning seems to have been ignored as the committee met in Wynn's on a number of occasions to plan the public inauguration of the 'Irish Volunteers'.

The Foundation of Cumann na mBan

On the 2nd April 1914 the inaugural public meeting of Cumann na mBan ~ The Irish Woman's Council, an Irish Republican Women's Paramilitary organisation was held in Wynn's Hotel. It was presided over by Agnes O'Farrell who was elected president.

The provisional executive unveiled at the meeting included; Jennie Wyse Power, Nancy O'Rahilly, Agnes MacNeill, Mary Colum, Nurse McCoy, Margaret Dobbs, Louise Gavin Duffy and Elizabeth Bloxham. Thus merging

and dissolving Iníon na hÉireann. During The Rising of Easter week 1916 it became an auxiliary of the Irish Volunteers. Although it was otherwise an independent organisation, its executive was subordinate to that of the volunteers.

The first branch was named the Ard Chraobh, which held their meetings in Brunswick Street, before and after the 1916 Easter Rising. The constitution of Cumann na mBan contained explicit references to the use of force by arms if necessary. At the time the Government of Ireland Bill 1914 was being debated, and might have had to be enforced in Ulster. The primary aims of the organization as stated in its constitution were to "advance the cause of Irish liberty and to organise Irishwomen in the furtherance of this object", to "assist in arming and equipping a body of Irish men for the defence of Ireland" and to "form a fund for these purposes, to be called 'The Defence of Ireland Fund'".

Picture Number 5:

Lower Abbey Street, showing the Royal Hibernian Academy & The Wynn Hotel

View From Abbey Street, Looking North East

In addition to their local subscriptions (i.e. involvement in other nationalist associations or organizations), members of Cumann na mBan were expected to support the Defence of Ireland Fund, through subscription or otherwise. Its recruits were from diverse backgrounds, mainly white collar workers and professional women, but with a significant proportion also from the working class. In September 1914, the Irish Volunteers split over John Redmond's appeal for its members to enlist in the British Army. The majority of Cumann na mBan members supported the 10,000 - 14,000 volunteers who rejected this call and who retained the original name, the Irish Volunteers.

The involvement of Cumann na mBan in the 1916 Rising:

On 23rd April 1916, when the Military Council of the IRB finalized arrangements for the Easter Rising, it integrated Cumann na mBan, along with the Irish Volunteers and the Irish Citizen Army, into the 'Army of the Irish Republic'. Pádraig Pearse was appointed overall Commandant-General and James Connolly Commandant-General of the Dublin Division.

On the day of the Rising, Cumann na mBan members, including Winifred Carney, who arrived, armed with both a Webley Revolver and a typewriter entered the General Post Office on O'Connell Street in Dublin with their male counterparts. By nightfall, women insurgents were established in the entire major rebel strongholds throughout the city – bar two, Boland's Mill and the South Dublin Union held by Éamon De Valera and Eamonn Ceannt respectively.

The majority of the women worked as Red Cross workers, were couriers, or procured rations for the men. Members also gathered intelligence on scouting expeditions, carried dispatches and transferred arms from dumps across the city to insurgent strongholds.

Markievicz, Mary Hyland and Lily Kempson were Cumann na mBan members amongst a force of twelve led by Frank Robbins who raided Trinity College, and found fifty rifles; but by that time the Green garrison had retreated to a smaller, but stronger building, the College of Surgeons.

Helena Maloney was among the soldiers who attacked Dublin Castle, where she worked with the wounded. A number of Cumann na mBan members died in the Rising.

At the Four Courts they helped to organise the evacuation of buildings at the time of surrender and to destroy incriminating papers. This was exceptional; more typical was the General Post Office (GPO), where Pearse insisted that most of them (excluding Carney, who refused to leave the injured James Connolly leave at noon on Friday, 28th April. The building was then coming under sustained shell and machine-gun fire, and heavy casualties were anticipated. The following day the leaders at the GPO decided to negotiate surrender. Pearse asked Cumann Na mBan member Elizabeth O' Farrell to act as a go-between.

Under British military supervision she brought Pearse's surrender order to the rebel units still fighting in Dublin. Over 70 women, including many of the leading figures in Cumann Na mBan, were arrested after the Insurrection, and many of the women who had been captured fighting were imprisoned in Kilmainham; all but 12 had been released by 8th May 1916.

George Oliver Plunkett, brother of proclamation signatory Joseph Plunkett.

George Oliver Plunkett

At 26 Upper Fitzwilliam Street Dublin, George Oliver Plunkett (also known as Seoirse Plunkett) was born on the 5th July 1894. He was the fifth child and second son of Count George Noble Plunkett and his wife Josephine Plunkett. Like his elder brother Joseph, George enjoyed the trappings of a wealthy upper-class childhood. He was educated at Belvedere College in Dublin and then was sent to Stonyhurst College in Lancashire where he trained as a military officer. On returning to Dublin, he began studying Dentistry at University College Dublin until his involvement in the Easter Rising resulted in imprisonment.

Sharing his elder brother's nationalist ideals, George had joined the Volunteers in 1914 where he rose to become a Captain. His duties included commanding the seventy men who enlisted in the IVF after they returned from Britain to avoid wartime conscription. The group became known as the 'Kimmage garrison' on account of them residing at the Plunkett's family estate Larkfield, situated at Kimmage in Co. Dublin. There, the men trained and learned how to use military weapons, including bombs ahead of the forthcoming Rising. Allegedly, George was also responsible in helping his brother Joseph and friend Rory O'Connor to produce and print the forged 'Castle document'. This document was initially said to have been in code and spirited out of Dublin Castle by a nationalist sympathiser as it listed a number of 'precautionary measures' that would be taken by British authorities to suppress republican activities. Later critics would argue that the Plunkett's and O'Connor had forged the document so as to convince Eoin MacNeill that the Rising should go ahead.

George along with his two brothers Joseph and Jack, spent Easter Week fighting in the GPO. He was applauded for his humanity during the evacuation of the GPO on Friday 28th April as he came to the assistance of a British soldier trapped between friendly fire on Moore Street. Following surrender, he was arrested, court-martialled and sentenced to death. Owing to the public outpouring of sympathy for the Plunkett family following the execution of Joseph and the arrest of the elderly Count and Countess Plunkett, his and Jack's sentences were reduced to 10 years penal servitude. His sister Geraldine later described how even the authorities empathised with the family during their difficult time:

"When the newspapers came out on Saturday the 6th (May 1916) we saw that George and Jack had also been sentenced to death and the sentence commuted to ten years. Jack told me afterwards that he had been told first of the death sentence and that the officer had then paused for a whole minute before telling him it had been commuted. Jack and George were

brought to Moutnjoy Jail for a few days, and then brought in a cattle boat to Holyhead. They spent six months in Portland prison before being moved to Pankhurst, on the Isle of Wight. I got some South African medal ribbon because it was green, white and orange and made it into a bow which I wore everywhere. A big policeman in Dame Street stopped me and said the tricolour would get me into trouble. I said, 'I have one brother shot and two brothers sentenced to death and my father and mother in jail. He said 'You're Plunkett, you can wear it'. "

Released in 1917, George would continue to play an active role in the republican movement.

OBLACHT NA H EIREANN

THE PROVISIONAL GOVERNMENT

OF THE

IRISH REPUBLIC

TO THE PEOPLE OF IRELAND.

IRISHMEN AND IRISHWOMEN: In the name of God and of the dead generations from which she receives her old tradition of nationhood, Ireland, through us, summons her children to her flag and strikes for her freedom.

Having organised and trained her manhood through her secret revolutionary organisation, the Irish Republican Brotherhood, and through her open military organisations, the Irish Volunteers and the Irish Citizen Army, having patiently perfected her discipline, having resolutely waited for the right moment to reveal itself, she now seizes that moment, and, supported by her exiled children in America and by gallant allies in Europe, but relying in the first on her own strength, she strikes in full confidence of victory.

We declare the right of the people of Ireland to the ownership of Ireland, and to the unfettered control of Irish destinies, to be sovereign and indefeasible. The long usurpation of that right by a foreign people and government has not extinguished the right, nor can it ever be extinguished except by the destruction of the Irish people. In every generation the Irish people have asserted their right to national freedom and sovereignty; six times during the past three hundred years they have asserted it in arms. Standing on that fundamental right and again asserting it in arms in the face of the world, we hereby proclaim the Irish Republic as a Sovereign Independent State, and we pledge our lives and the lives of our comrades-in-arms to the cause of its freedom, of its welfare, and of its exaltation among the nations.

The Irish Republic is entitled to, and hereby claims, the allegiance of every Irishman and Irishwoman. The Republic guarantees religious and civil liberty, equal rights and equal opportunities to all its citizens, and declares its resolve to pursue the happiness and prosperity of the whole nation and of all its parts, cherishing all the children of the nation equally, and oblivious of the differences carefully fostered by an alien government, which have divided a minority from the majority in the past.

Until our arms have brought the opportune moment for the establishment of a permanent National Government, representative of the whole people of Ireland and elected by the suffrages of all her men and women, the Provisional Government, hereby constituted, will administer the civil and military affairs of the Republic in trust for the people.

We place the cause of the Irish Republic under the protection of the Most High God, Whose blessing we invoke upon our arms, and we pray that no one who serves that cause will dishonour it by cowardice, inhumanity, or rapine. In this supreme hour the Irish nation must, by its valour and discipline and by the readiness of its children to sacrifice themselves for the common good, prove itself worthyof the august destiny to which it is called.

Signed on Behalf of the Provisional Government,

THOMAS J. CLARKE,
SEAN Mac DIARMADA. THOMAS MacDONAGH,
P. H. PEARSE, EAMONN CEANNT,
JAMES CONNOLLY. JOSEPH PLUNKETT.

Lower Sackville Street/ Nelson's Pillar:

Sackville Street was laid out and built in the 1750s by Luke Gardiner on land that had previously been the property of St. Mary's Abbey. No expense was spared in the construction of the street because the residents of Sackville Street were typically members of the Irish Parliament and therefore very wealthy. Many of these MP's employed the best architects of the day to build and design their properties. Owing to this the architecture of the east side of the street, (where the wealthiest men in the neighbourhood lived) was superior to that of the west side, where speculative builders and architects built houses in the hope of then selling them. Located closely to the Rotunda Hospital, Sackville Street became one of the most fashionable parts of Dublin to live in.

The street continued to develop during the course of the 19th century and the GPO, designed by Francis Johnston, was constructed during the years 1814-1818. It was to be the most important building built by Johnston in Dublin and arguably one of the most expensive of his creations as construction costs were estimated to have totalled over £50,000. Styled like many of the Georgian public buildings in Dublin in the Graeco-Roman style, the main facade was decorated with a clock and a peal of bells (later removed to Earlsfort Terrace) and the three figures of Fidelity, Hibernia and Mercury (scuplted by Cork born scupltor Thomas Kirk) stood on top of the pediment.

By the end of the 19th century, Sackville Street was a busy commercial street. Census records indicate that every building along the street had a commercial purpose, ranging from hotels to jewellers, booksellers to boot makers and china shops to military outfitters. Easter Monday in

1916 found the street as lively as ever as the bank holiday crowds mulled around Dublin's city centre enjoying the good weather. Few could have imagined that within six days the GPO would be gutted and the lower end of Sackville Street utterly destroyed. The properties located at the upper end of the street managed to survive the Rising, but commercial businesses were looted and had their windows and interiors destroyed by the inhabitants of the nearby slums. The streets located in the area around Sackville Street were also damaged due to the spread of fire and the indirect shelling by the British authorities.

Consequently commercial life in this part of inner Dublin was greatly impaired. Many businesses had lost not only their premises but also their stock and had no option but to shut down. Others were forced to remain closed for six years as the rebuilding process did not begin until peace was restored after the establishment of the Irish Free State in 1922. A lucky few were able to rent temporary premises elsewhere and in the weeks and months after the Rising, they spent considerable money advertising their temporary move in the commercial Dublin papers.

An advisory committee was appointed late in 1916 to oversee and control the rebuilding of Sackville Street. Town planners, including Dublin City architect C.J. McCarthy recognised the opportunity to modernise the entire street and they drafted 'The Dublin Reconstruction (Emergency Provisions) Act, 1916'. Today Sackville Street is named O'Connell Street, after the Irish poliitician Daniel O'Connell.

Henry Street - Looking East to Nelson's Pillar

Nelson's Pillar:

Three years after the Battle of Trafalgar (1805), the Nelson Pillar was built to commemorate the victory of Lord Nelson. It was deemed an appropriate subject for Dublin's main street because the victory had opened up sea routes to the Continent, which had benefited Dublin trade. The pillar was located on the spot where the Upper street and Lower street met and at the cross axis with Henry Street and Earl Street. The pillar, a large Portland granite doric column was twice the height of the street's buildings and stood at 134 feet. A scuplture of Horatio Nelson stood atop the Pillar. Commissioned by the Lord Mayor of Dublin, James Vance, the sculpture was executed by Thomas Kirk. Unveiled in 1809 the Pillar survived the Rising but was destroyed after a bomb attack by the Irish Republican Army (IRA) in 1966.

The Metropole Hotel

Situated next to the GPO, The Metropole Hotel was one of the best hotels in Dublin. With 100 bedrooms, lit by electricity and with a working electric 'passenger lift', the Metropole was a well known and much loved landmark on Lower Sackville Street. Unsurprisingly Easter weekend found the hotel busy with visitors and guests. When the Rising began on Easter Monday afternoon the hotel staff did their best to protect their guests from the events unfolding.

On Tuesday 25th April, Oscar Traynor and his battalion were instructed by the Provisional Government to seize all the shops and premises from the Hotel

Metropole to the corner of Abbey Street. Entering the Metropole they ordered the guests and staff to leave, and took some British army officers who were staying in the hotel prisoner. They then set about fortifying the hotel by digging through interior walls, erecting barricades and posting men at the windows to oversee the drama unfolding outside.

From the Tuesday evening until Friday the 25th, when the Volunteers were ordered to return to the GPO to receive orders from Pearse, the Metropole came under heavy fire from the British authorities. Following the dispatch of the Volunteers occupying the hotel, the same fire which destroyed the GPO swept through the Metropole on Friday night. Unable to extinguish it, the grand hotel burned to the ground. In the aftermath of the Rising one journalist estimated that the damage caused to the commercial premises on Sackville Street alone totaled £241,870 of the overall £2.5 million worth of damage incurred in Dublin as a result of the rebellion.

The Metropole hotel would not be rebuilt. Instead a luxurious entertainment complex was built on the original site, complete with a cinema, a dancehall and a restaurant. The Metropole cinema opened in 1922, with the capacity to seat 1,000 people, at its height the cinema employed over 200 people before its closure in 1972.

Thomas Mac Donagh:

Born on the 1st February 1878 in Cloughjordan, Co Tipperary to Joseph and Mary MacDonagh, Thomas was their third child and the eldest son of their six children who would survive childhood. Both parents were national schoolteachers and they installed their children with a love of music and literature. Having been taught his primary education by his father, MacDonagh would enter Rockwell College, Cashel, Co. Tipperary in 1892 with the intention of becoming a priest. However after realising that the religious life was not for him, he abandoned the priesthood to be a teacher and writer. He was employed by St. Kierans College in Kilkenny as an English, French and History teacher from 1901-1903 and it was during this tenure that he first attended a Gaelic League meeting. Later he would refer to this initial meeting as his 'baptism in nationalism' and he chose to join the Kilkenny branch of the Gaelic League. Through attending summer language courses on Inishmaan, Co. Galway MacDonagh became a fluent Irish speaker and writer, a talent which he demonstrated when he wrote his two first volumes of poetry - *Through the ivory gate* and *April and May* in 1903.

Picture Number 8:

MacDonagh would move to Cork in 1903 after being employed by St. Colman's College in Fermoy, where he would remain until 1908. During his time in Cork, his interest in the Gaelic League continued and he formed a new branch of the League while there. His move to Dublin in 1908 brought him into closer contact with leading nationalists such as Eoin MacNeill and Patrick Pearse who he was already acquainted with. Impressed by Pearse's ambitions of founding a boys school

which would encourage students to become billingual in English and Irish, MacDonagh became the resident assistant headmaster and instructor of Language and Literature of St. Enda's. MacDonagh also became active in Dublin's theatrical circles, forming a close friendship with Joseph Plunkett and availing of theopportunity to write and stage nationalist plays in the Abbey Theatre.

Having completed his Masters in English at University College Dublin in October 1911, MacDonagh was appointed a full-time assistant lecturer in English in the university, which prompted him to leave St. Enda's. His interest in nationalism and the Gaelic revival persisted however, even after his marriage to Muriel Gifford (sister of Grace Gifford, the future wife of Joseph Plunkett) in 1912. The couple initially resided at 32 Baggot Street but following the births of their two children Donagh and Barbara, they moved to 29 Oakley Road, Ranelagh.

In 1913 MacDonagh attended the inaugral meeting of the IVF. Though initially keen not to engage in violence, his stance had altered in the wake of witnessing the conduct of the Dublin Metropolitan Police towards the general public and the striking workers, during the 1913 Dublin Lockout. The outbreak of the First World War convinced him of the necessity of staging an uprising while British authorities' atttention was distracted with the war ongoing in Europe.

MacDonagh played a limited role in preparations for the Rising. While he had been inauguarated into the IRB in March 1915 and had played a prominent role in organising the funeral of O'Donnovan Rossa, he was not informed of the plans for the upcoming Rising until a few weeks prior to it occurring. As the last of the seven signatories added on to the IRB military council, MacDonagh's role was quite limited during the final stages of the planning process. Primairly he acted as an intermediary between Eoin MacNeill and the other leaders of the Rising.

During the Rising he commanded the Jacob's Factory garrison and the 170 men and women who comprised his rank and file Volunteers. He and his officers had very limited military experience, so they were quite grateful to Major John McBride who had joined the Volunteers campaign on Easter Monday morning. The factory witnessed very little fighting and only surrendered on Sunday 30th April after they recieved Pearse's orders.

MacDonagh was court-martialled on the 2nd May in Richmond Barracks and was charged with taking part in an armed rebellion 'with the intention and for the purpose of assisting the enemy'. Described by his prosecutor as 'a poet, a dreamer and an idealist', MacDonagh never spoke during his trial - the only individual of all those court-martialled not to do so. Found guilty, he was executed early on the morning of the 3rd May.

Thomas James Clarke:

Thomas (Tom) Clarke was the eldest of four children born to James Clarke, an Anglican bombardier in the Royal Artillery and his wife Mary. The family spent 8 years in South Africa due to James' career, they returned to Ireland and settled in Dungannon, Co. Tyrone in 1867. Clarke was educated in St. Patrick's national school in Dungannon and became a monitor there after he completed his academic education. His political education began in earnest after John Daly's visit to Dungannon in 1878. Daly was a national organiser for the IRB and his speech had such a profound impact on Clarke that he joined the Dungannon IRB and became the branch's first district secretary.

He was forced to emigrate to New York in 1880 after he attempted to shoot at memebrs of the local police force during a riot in Dungannon. In New York, where he was employed as a hotel porter, Clarke joined Clan na Gael and began attending Dr. Thomas Gallagher's bomb-making classes. Befriending his instructor, Clarke would travel to London in March 1883 along with Gallagher with the intent of conducting a bombing mission in the British capital. Instead, they were arrested after suspicions were raised over the heavy black bag which Clarke carried with him. On 11th June 1883 Clarke was convicted of treason-felony and sentenced to a lifetime of penal servitude. Treason convictons were taken very seriously in the prisons where he served his sentence, (Millbank, Chatham and Portland). Prisoners had a servere regime of hard labour, little exercise and enforced silence imposed on them- with the result that many of them went insane. Clarke maintained his sanity thanks to his friendship with fellow Feninan prisoner John Daly and James Francis Egan, all three developed ingenious ways of comunicating with one another and their friendship survived for the rest of their lives.

T.J.CLARK.

KEOGH BROS. DUBLIN.

After appeals from the Amenesty Association, Clarke was eventually released on 29th September 1898, having served 15 years of his sentence. Prison had taken his toll on him and his appearance - he was stooped and prematurely aged - but his nationalist militant beliefs remained intact. Settling with his mother and sister in Kilmainham, Dublin, Clarke found it difficult to gain employment, so he once again emigrated to New York in 1900. He found work with Clan na Gael and married John Daly's niece Kathleen, who had left her thriving dressmaking business in Limerick to move to New York to be with him. Major John MacBride, who would later be executed for his role in

the 1916 Rising, acted as Clarke's best man. In September 1903, Clarke helped launch the *Gaelic American* magazine, of which he was the assistant editor, but due to ill health he would resign from the magazine two years later. Having become naturalised American citizen on 2nd November 1905, he and his family moved to Manorville in Long Island where he ran a market garden farm.

In 1907, the Clarke family returned to Ireland and by February 1908, Clarke had opened a tobacconist and newsagent at on Amiens Street, in 1909 he would open another shop on Parnell Street. The shop on Parnell Street become the hub of IRB activity within Dublin city over the next few years. Clarke's return to Ireland coincided with a movement within the IRB to revitalise the organisation. With his long history of involvement in Fenian activity, Clarke was revered by younger members of the IRB, especially Seán MacDermott who would become his right-hand man during 1910/1911. The two men, in conjuncion with Denis McCullough and Bulmer Hobson began publishing the republican journal *Irish Freedom* from the 15th November 1910 until it was suppressed in December 1914. Keen to be active in all apsects of the Irish nationalist movement, Clarke joined the Gaelic League and Sinn Féin. In 1913 he also helped establish the IVF, as he recognised the potential of having a large body of nationalist militia available for any future rebellions. On the 9th September 1914 following the oubreak of the First World War and the internal split within the Volunteers, Clarke chaired the meeting of a number of IRB members where it was decided to begin planning for the Rising.

Dublin Castle regarded Clarke to be the brains of the nationalist movement and they were right. Of all the characters involved in the Rising, few did more than Clarke who, until he was accidently shot in the arm during an IVF military drill in January 1916, worked diligently to make preparations for the landing of German arms in Ireland. His fellow signatories of the Proclamation recognised this dedication when signing, as they insisted on Clarke's signature being the first on the document.

Over the course of Easter Week, Clarke held no official position or military rank in the GPO, but the repsonsibility of presiding over the military council meetings which occurred after Connolly was shot, fell to him. Eager to die for the cause, Clarke was the only one of the leaders who rejected the suggestion to surrender, but he was overruled. After surrendering, Clarke was held in front of the Rotunda alongside the other surrendered Volunteers. Identified by British officer Captain P.S. Lea-Wilson as the chief ringleader, Clarke was subjected to humiliating verbal abuse and was roughly stripped of his clothing. Later during the War of Independence, Lea-Wilson, now employed as a RIC officer, would be shot as punishment for his behaviour towards Clarke. Court-martialled on the 2nd May, Clarke would be executed on the morning of the 3rd May and subsequently buried at Arbour Hill. During the course of his final meeting with his wife, Clarke is said to have predicted that between the Rising and Ireland eventually achieving freedom, 'Ireland will go through hell, but she will never lie down again until she has attained full freedom'.

The Irish Proclamation issued by the rebels of the Easter 1916 Rising

The Proclamation of the Irish Republic (also known as *'Poblacht na h-Éireann'*) was issued by the Volunteers and the ICA on Easter Monday and was read aloud by Patrick Pearse on the steps of the GPO.

The document was addressed from the 'Provisional Government of the Irish Republic' (the self-styled title devised by the IRB's secret military council to refer to themselves) to the 'people of Ireland' and it proclaimed Ireland's independence from the United Kingdom.

Modelled on a similar independence proclamation issued by Robert Emmet during his 1803 rebellion, the document drew on the historical tradition of rebellion in Ireland by alluding to Wolfe Tone and the United Irishmen. It stated that 'In every generation the Irish people have asserted their right to national freedom and sovereignty; six times during the past three hundred years thay have asserted it in arms'.

The Proclamation also referenced Ireland's diaspora, who were described as 'exiled children in America' and included a number of religious references. For instance the opening words of the Proclamation were 'In the name of God' and the concluding paragraph began with the phrase, 'We place the cause of the Irish Republic under the protection of the Most High God, Whose blessing we invoke upon our arms'.

Full of heroic language the Proclamation did not initially have the impact that the Provisional Goverment had hoped for. Those who listened as Pearse read the document aloud were bemused and some sniggered as James Connolly shook Pearse's hand and congratulated him after he had finished. Few realised that by signing the Proclamation, the seven signatories had resigned themselves to accept what the final line described as the need for some 'to sacrifice themselves for the common good'.

The Proclamation also definitively stated that:

- The 1916 Easter Rising marked yet another attempt to achieve Irish independence from 'foreign rule' through the use of arms.
- The IRB, the Volunteers and the ICA were central to the planning and staging of the Rising.
- The Rising had international support in America and Europe.
- The Provisional Government would administer the civil and military affairs of the Republic for the Irish people.

Arguably, the Proclamation along with the tricolour and the GPO are the three most identifiable symbols of the Easter Rising and all three continue to play an important role in commemorating the event.

The principles of the proclamation:

While the Rising eventually ended in failure, the Proclamation survived and its principles have continued to influence the ideas and ideologies of Irish politicians ever since. The Proclamation also provided a basic framework of what people should expect of an independent Ireland including:

- The idea that the people of Ireland had 'the right' to ownership of Ireland.

- The form of government would be a 'Republic'

- The fact that a permanent National Government would be formed 'representative of the whole people of Ireland' and 'elected by the suffrages of all her men and women'. Meaning that the Republic would commit to Universal suffrage for its people.

- The idea that the Irish Republic was 'entitled to' and would claim the 'allegiance of every Irishman and Irishwoman'.

- The assertion that the Irish Republic would guarantee 'religious and civil liberty, equal rights and equal opportunities to all its citizens'. In other words, the Republic would strive to end sectarianism and encourage gender equality.

- The promise that 'all the children of the nation' (Nationalists and Unionists) would be cherished equally within the Republic.

The Proclamation of the Irish Republic was shaped by the ambitions and political ideologies of its signatories. They in turn drew their inspiration from politics (especially in the case of James Connolly and his socialist beliefs) and from the Gaelic revival and Irish nationalist movement which had developed around the turn of the century. Ultimately the leaders desired to delve into Ireland's historic past and recreate a free, Gaelic and egalitarian Ireland

POBLACHT NA H E

THE PROVISIONAL GOVE

OF THE

IRISH REPU

TO THE PEOPLE OF IRE

IRISHMEN AND IRISHWOMEN: In the name of God and of
from which she receives her old tradition of nationhood, Ireland,
her children to her flag and strikes for her freedom.
Having organised and trained her manhood through her s
organisation, the Irish Republican Brotherhood, and through
organisations, the Irish Volunteers and the Irish Citizen Arm
perfected her discipline, having resolutely waited for the right
itself, she now seizes that moment, and, supported by her exiled c
and by gallant allies in Europe, but relying in the first on her o
strikes in full confidence of victory.
We declare the right of the people of Ireland to the ownership o
the unfettered control of Irish destinies, to be sovereign and indefeas
usurpation of that right by a foreign people and government has not
right, nor can it ever be extinguished except by the destruction of the I
every generation the Irish people have asserted their right to nation
sovereignty; six times during the past three hundred years they have
arms. Standing on that fundamental right and again asserting it in
of the world, we hereby proclaim the Irish Republic as a Sov
and we pledge our lives and the lives of our comrades
of its welfare, and of its exaltation amo
The Irish Republi
Irishman and

The Signatories:

Seven signatories names appeared on the *Proclamation of the Irish Republic*. They were:

- Thomas J Clarke
- Seán MacDermott
- Thomas MacDonagh
- P.H. Pearse
- Éamonn Ceannt
- James Connolly
- Joseph Plunkett

All of the signatories would later be executed for playing a role in the Rising and for devising the Proclamation - a document which was considered treason by British authorities. Especially as it was devised and printed during the First World War and referred to the Irish Republic being supported by 'gallant allies in Europe', which the British authorities interpreted to mean Germany.

The content of the document had been agreed upon by the signatories when they had met at 21 Henry Street, the home of John and Henny Wyse-Powe and everyone, except the ill Joseph Plunkett, gathered at the house on the Tuesday before the Rising to sign the proclamation. Plunkett would officially sign the document on Easter Sunday morning in Liberty Hall- after it had been set by the printers with his name on it. Owing to the fact that the official Proclamation was printed in Liberty Hall on Easter Sunday, the signatories are said to have signed an ordinary piece of paper, and then the printers simply printed their signatures on to the final document.

Three men, Christopher Brady, Michael Molly and Liam F. O'Brien and one woman, Roseanne (Rosie) Hackett were responsible for typing and printing the Proclamation. The men had all worked for printing companies, Hackett had not-instead she had been employed in the Jacobs factory but had been unemployed since the 1913 Dublin Lockout. In order to prevent the men getting in trouble with the authorities for printing the proclamation, Connolly had them 'arrested' when they arrived at Liberty Hall. This meant that they could later admit under oath that they had participated in printing the document under 'duress' and therefore could not be tried for treason.

The printing press used to produce the proclamation was an old Wharfedale Double-Crown, which was in very poor condition. As the printers did not have enough font to use, the document had to be run through the printing press twice. The first three paragraphs were printed first, then the type was broken up and reset for the rest of the document. It was this section that was discovered in the press when the British military seized Liberty Hall on 27th April 1916. They printed off a number of these 'half' copies and they were used in the trials as evidence against the Rising's leaders. Very few copies of the Proclamation survived the Rising owing to the small number that was printed (1,000 in total) and the poor quality of the paper used.

Background on the other Signatories:

Éamonn Ceannt

Edward Thomas Kent was born on 21st September 1881 in Ballymoe, Glenamaddy, Co. Galway, the sixth boy of seven children born to Royal Irish Constabulary (RIC) Constable James Kent and his wife Johanna. In 1883 the family moved to Ardee Co. Louth, where Edward attended the local De La Salle national school. The family subsequently moved to Drogheda and Edward attended the local CBS School in 1888. Edward would complete his studies at O'Connell's CBS, North Richmond Street in Dublin, after his father retired from the RIC.

Ceannt and the Gaelic League.

Working as a clerk in the city's treasury office of Dublin Corporation, Kent's interest in cultural nationalism was sparked by the commemorations for the 1798 rebellion. Having been tutored in Irish by his father (a fluent Gaelic speaker) he joined the Gaelic League in September 1899 and adopted the Gaelic version of his name, 'Éamonn Ceannt'. Through the Gaelic League, he met his wife Francis Mary O'Brennan (also known as Áine) who he married on the 7th June 1905 in Dublin's St. James' Church. They moved to 2 Dolphin's Terrace, South Circular Road and their son Ronan was born in 1906. By 1909 Ceannt was fluent in Irish and was teaching classes for Gaelic League members. During the course of 1909 he had also been elected on to the Gaelic

League's governing body. His interest in politics and nationalism continued to develop during the first decade of the 20th century, reflected in his participation in demonstrations against George V's planned royal visit to Dublin in 1911. Having belonged to Sinn Féin since 1907, Ceannt became increasingly militant in his beliefs and became close to Seán MacDermott who recruited him into the IRB in 1911. On MacDermott's insistence, Ceannt became a founding member of the Volunteers in 1913. Serving as a Captain in the IVF, Ceannt participated in the Howth and Kilcoole gun-running's in 1914. Chosen to become a member of the IRB supreme council in 1915, Ceannt would subsequently join the IRB's secret military council. It was his job to keep other moderate Volunteer leaders (who were not in favour of militant violence) in the dark about the plans for a Rising.

The Easter Rising:

When the Rising did occur, Ceannt was put in command of the South Dublin Union, with around 100 men under him– including Cathal Brugha and (future President of the Irish Free State's Executive Council) W.T. Cosgrave. The Union was close to a number of the British army barracks and over the course of Easter week the Volunteers stationed there witnessed some of the bloodiest fighting of any of the rebel garrisons. Adhering to Pearse's orders, Ceannt and his men surrendered on the Saturday afternoon. During his court martial at Richmond Barracks, Ceannt defended himself so eloquently that the press initially reported he had only received a three year prison sentence. In reality he was found guilty on the 6th May and was executed by firing squad on the 8th May in Kilmainham Jail.

Séan Mac Diarmada (Mac Dermott)

Born in January 1883 and baptised on the 29th January in Corranmore, Kiltyclougher, Co. Leitrim, Seán MacDermott was the eighth child born to carpenter Donald McDermott and his wife Mary. Educated at Corracloona national school, MacDermott had initially wished to become a teacher, but his poor

maths skills caused him to fail to qualify for a teaching scholarship. Having briefly emigrated in 1904 and worked as a gardner in Edinburgh, he returned to Ireland in 1905 and studied bookkeeping, shorthand and Irish at night school in Dowra Co. Cavan. He secured a job as a tramcar conductor in Belfast in 1905. However, he was dismissed in 1906 due to being caught smoking on the tram platform.

Convinced that Ireland's future required a militant and physical rebellion against the British, he had come into contact with some Belfast members of the IRB and was subsequently sworn into the IRB in Belfast on the recommendation of Denis McCullogh, a close friend of Bulmer Hobson. MacDermott was employed as the chief organiser of the Dungannon Clubs (an organisation open to anyone, founded by Hobson and McCullogh to promote nationalism in Ulster). In April 1907, the Dungannon Clubs amalgamated with Arthur Griffith's Cummann na nGaedheal organisation to form the Sinn Féin League, MacDermott's employment was transferred to this new organisation. An enthusiastic cyclist and an early supporter of the motorcar, MacDermott was responsible for the foundation of Sinn Féin branches throughout Ireland. He also began secretly recruiting men to join the IRB after he was appointed as the IRB's national organiser in 1908. It was his responsibility to oversee the infilitration of national cultural organisations, such as the Gaelic Athletic Association (GAA) by the IRB. In 1911 he was elected on to the IRB's Supreme Council.

Struck down with polio for much of the winter of 1911 and the spring of 1912, when he recovered he was left permanently partially disabled in his right leg and he took to walking with the aid of a stick. His close relationship with Tom Clarke and their shared belief in the need for militant action, prompted MacDermott's enthusiastic support for the IVF and he attended their initial meeting in Wynn's Hotel on the 11th November 1913. As a paid organiser for the Volunteers from 1914 onwards he travelled extensively in Ireland recruiting men to join the IVF and secretly placing IRB members in high-ranking positions within the IVF organisation.

The Rising owed a great deal to MacDermott who oversaw many of the logistical preparations, including the temporary confinement of Bulmer Hobson on Good Friday. During the Rising he remained in the GPO and acted as adjunct to Connolly. After Connolly was injured, MacDermott and Clarke took increasing control of the Volunteer's miltary campaign. It was MacDermott who read Pearse's order of surrender aloud to the remaining Volunteers residing on Moore Street on Saturday the 29th April. Inspite of his disability, MacDermott marched to the Rotunda hospital, where he was held captive outside overnight with the rest of the surrendered Volunteers. He was then marched to Richmond barracks where he was identified as a leader of the Rising. Court martialled on the 9th May, he and Connolly were the last of the leaders to be executed on the morning of the 12th May.

Joseph Mary Plunkett

Born on the 21st November 1887 at 26 Upper Fitzwilliam Street to Count and Countess Plunkett, Joseph was the second child and the eldest son of the seven Plunkett children. While they enjoyed a priviliged upbring, the difficult personalities of his parents had a lasting impact on all their children, specifically Joseph who developed a rather eccentric and nervous personality. His chronic ill health - during childhood he suffered from pleurisy, pneumonia and glandular tuberculosis (TB) - exacerbated his nervous disposition. Educated at the Catholic University School on Leeson Street, he was briefly educated in Paris, before returning to Dublin and enrolling in Belvedere College. During his teenage years bouts of ill-health meant he was often confined to the family home so private home tutors were hired in order for his education to continue. After attending Stonyhurst College in Lanchasire for two years, where he studied philosophy, he returned to Ireland keen to study at University College Dublin.

Preparations for the University College Dublin matriculation exams brought him into contact with Thomas MacDonagh who became a close friend. Ill health forced him to spend time abroad in 1911 and 1912 visiting Italy, Sicily, Malta and later Algiers. Returning to Ireland in 1912, he fell ill with influenza, suffered lung haemorrhages and spent several months in hospital. On recovering, he moved in with his sister Geraldine at 17 Marlborough Road, Donnybrook. The Dublin Lockout in 1913 introduced Plunkett to public affairs and politics, which resulted in him offering his services to Eoin MacNeill when the IVF were launched. Utilising the *Irish Review*, a literary magazine which he owned and edited, Plunkett regularly exalted the Volunteers among the pages of the

publication, in an attempt to encourage and popularise IVF membership. Countess Plunkett's large property portfolio proved exceptionaly useful for her son's nationalist ambitions and he launched his, MacDonagh and the dramatist Edward Martyn's theatre company, 'Irish Theatre' in Hardwicke Hall in 1914.

Opposing Redmond's ambition that the Volunteers would support the British war effort, Plunkett attended the secret meeting held in the Gaelic League headquarters on the 20th September 1914 with other IRB members including Clarke, MacDermott and MacDonagh during which it was agreed that an uprising would be staged while the war continued in mainland Europe. Owing to his military knowledge (the result of officer training at Stonyhurst), Plunkett was inducted into the IRB and appointed the IRB's Director of Military Operations. This role led to him travelling to Germany in April 1915 where he joined the British diplomat - and enthusiastic Irish nationalist - Roger Casement in Berlin to try and muster German support and arms. The two men devised the *Ireland Report*, a hypothetical plan for an Irish rebellion intended for a German audience. The report provided details of what any potential German expeditionary force should expect to encounter in Ireland if they were to participate in a hypothetical rebellion. It also set out how the Volunteers intended to seize key buildings in Dublin during the course of their rebellion.

On returning to Ireland, he was appointed to the IRB's Military Council in May 1915 and the Plunkett family home at Larkfield in Kimmage effectively became an unofficial barracks for the 'Kimmage Garrison' and a store for military arms and ammunition. Ill health hampered Plunkett's involvement in the final preparations for Easter week. Having underwent surgery on his neck glands at the beginning of April, he did play a role in the forgery of the 'Dublin Castle document'. On Easter Sunday, he arrived to the Liberty Hall heavily bandaged but eager to participate. Remaining in the GPO for the duration of the Rising, he was assisted in his duties by his young aide-de-camp Michael Collins. Court-martialled on the 3rd May, Plunkett was granted permission to marry his fiancée Grace Gifford in the chapel of Kilmainham jail. Though seperated immediately after the service, the newlyweds were allowed ten minutes together in Plunkett's cell. Rumours the British authorities allowed the marriage ceremony to occur because Grace Gifford was pregnant have never been proven, though Plunkett's sister Geraldine would later claim Grace miscarried a few weeks after Plunkett's execution on the 4th May.

History Curriculum linked activities.

Strand: *Politics, conflict & Society*

Strand Unit: *1916 & the foundation of the State.*

Lesson objectives, as set out by the NCCA

The child should be enabled to;

- *engage in simple studies of some of the more important aspects of the 1916 Rising in which political changes or movements have had an important influence on the lives of people in Ireland*
- *acquire some knowledge of the major personalities, events or developments during the Rising.*
- *explore pictorial evidence, discuss, compare and develop some simple understanding of the attitudes, beliefs, motivations and actions of differing individuals and groups of people in the past*
- *begin to develop some appreciation of the 'mind-set' of former generations appreciate that the notion of tolerance developed over time, that the notion of equality of treatment of people had to evolve over time*
- *acquire insights into the attitudes and actions of people in contemporary Ireland.*

Picture Number 1: The General Post Office, taken from the book 'Six days after the Insurrection'.

1. On what Street was the GPO situated on during the 1916 Rising?
2. What did Patrick Pearse read aloud on the Steps of the GPO Easter Monday, April 24th1916?
3. Which of the Proclamation signatories led the rebels in fighting within the GPO?
4. Examining the photograph of the GPO, in your own words describe the events which took place there during Easter Week 1916?
5. Why do you think, did Patrick Pearse order a surrender?
6. Who negotiated Pearse's order of Surrender with General Lowe on Saturday 29th of April?

Picture No. 2: The Four Courts' Taken from the book 'Six days after the Insurrection'

1. Why do you think did the rebels lay siege in the Four Courts during the 1916 Rising?
2. Who led the volunteers in fighting within the Four Courts?
3. Describe the events of the first encounter with the British Army at the Four Courts?
4. Examining the Photograph, give an account in your own words of the fighting and rebellion which occurred there during Easter Week.
5. Researching some additional information, write a brief Biography on

Commander Ned (Edward)Daly

6. What did Ned Daly insist remain open for the local citizens?

Picture No. 3: The Royal College of Surgeons, Dublin.

1. Who was Michael Mallin's second in command during the Easter Rising of 1916?
2. Where were Mallin and Countess Marchievcz assigned to occupy during the Rising?
3. How did Mallin and his Volunteers attempt to fortify their position on St Stephens Green?
4. Who was Countess Markievicz and what was her role in the 1916 Rising?
5. Why do you think Mallin incriminated Countess Markievcz in his confession?
6. What happened to Commander Michael Mallin during the aftermath?

Picture No. 4: Liberty Hall.

1. Where is Liberty Hall situated within the capital city?
2. What was Liberty Hall used for during the Rising?
3. When did the Helga sail up the Liffey?
4. Describe in your own words the scene of the Helga shelling Liberty Hall.
5. Examining the Photograph, write a detailed account of the destruction the fighting around liberty hall caused during the Easter Rebellion.

Picture No.5: Lower Abbey Street

1. Examining the photograph, what buildings can be identified that were destroyed or damaged during the Easter Rising?
2. Name some of the patrons of Wynn's hotel prior to the Rising.
3. Who founded Cumann Na mBan and what was their involvement in the Rising?
4. Using your imagination, based on the pictorial evidence given, describe the scenes on Lower Abbey Street in the aftermath of the 1916 Rising.

Picture No. 6: The Irish Proclamation & signatories:

1. What was the purpose of the Irish Proclamation?
2. Looking at the photograph, list the seven signatories of the Proclamation in order of their signing?
3. Outline the principles of the Proclamation?
4. Describe how and where the Proclamation was prepared?

5. Why do you believe that Patrick Pearse's name was not the first name to appear as a signature on the proclamation?
6. Where can an original copy of the proclamation be seen in the present day?
7. Give a brief account of each of the seven Proclamation signatories?

Picture No. 7a /7b: Patrick Pearse & James Connolly

1. Where and when was Patrick Pearse born and give an account of his upbringing?
2. What did Patrick Pearse found in 1908?
3. What was his position within the IRB?
4. Where did Patrick Pearse read out the Irish Proclamation?
5. Describe in your own words, Pearse's role in the 1916 Rising.
6. Where and when was James Connolly born?
7. Who was Connolly Commander of during the 1916 rebellion?
8. Why was Connolly executed, whilst being seated on a chair?

Picture No. 8: Mac Donagh / Clarke

1. How did Mac Donagh befriend Patrick Pearse & the other rebel leaders?
2. Where was Mac Donagh's battalion stationed during the Easter Rising?
3. Who assisted MacDonagh within his battalion? And when did he decide to join the Rising?
4. Where and when was Thomas Clarke born?
5. Who did Clarke befriend during his time in prison?
6. Where was Clarke stationed during the 1916 Rising?
7. What did Thomas Clarke say to his wife during their final meeting?

Picture No. 9: Sackville St & Nelson's Pillar

1. By which name is Sackville Street now known and who was it named after?
2. What occurred on this street during the Easter Rising? Give a brief account of events.
3. Where did the rebels retreat to as the GPO went up in flames before surrendering?
4. Describe the destruction which the 1916 rebellion caused during the fighting of Easter Week?
5. When was Nelson's Pillar destroyed and by who?

Of all the rebellions staged during Ireland's long history, the Easter Rising is undoubtedly the one best documented. Letters and written correspondence was central to the planning and staging of the Rising and we are fortunate that a number of primary documents survived the Easter Rising. They provide us with a fascinating documentary of the events which unfolded during the course of Easter Week. As well as an insight into the psyche of many of the key individuals during the week long insurrection.

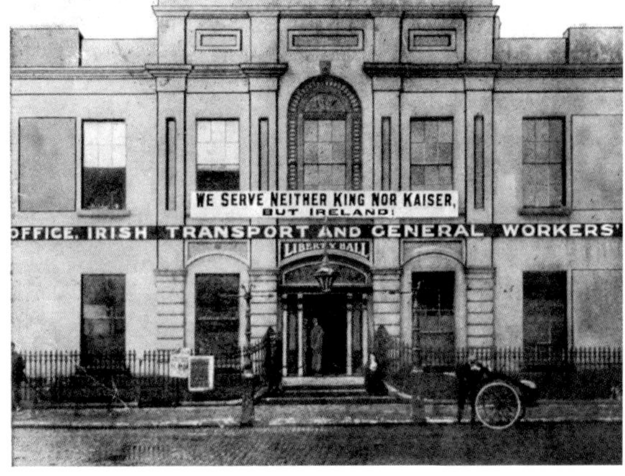

As Liberty Hall Appeared after the opening of the European War.

James Connolly's final memo

One such document was the final memo written by James Connolly as preparations were made to evacuate the burning GPO on Friday the 28th. Throughout the Rising the battalions posted around Dublin in the various garrisons had recieved written despatches relaying orders and updates from Connolly and Pearse. Rumours had already reached many of them that Connolly had been seriously injured late on Thursday and Connolly recognised that concern would grow when it became common knowledge that the GPO - the headquarters of the Provisional Government - had been evacuated. From his sick bed he dictated the following letter to his aide-de-camp and secretary Winfred Carney.

The overall tone of the letter was deliberately positive and he assured the Volunteers that both the Church and the lay population were unified in support of the Rising, something that was considered very important to the mainly Roman Catholic Volunteers but which in reality was most certainly not the case. The reference to the Dublin Brigade's Battalion (known as the 'Fingal Battalion') was overwhelmingly positive, in spite of the fact that the small force barely mustering

Liberty Hall, Headquarters of the Citizen Army, after bombardment.

Corner of Batchelors Walk and Lr. Sackville St. commanding O'Connell Bridge.

more than 40 men had only secured their success at Ashbourne aganist the local RIC as a result of luck and bluff.

This was the final update that many of the battalions recieved until Pearse's orders to surrender were delivered over the weekend. It is therefore understandable why so many Volunteers were shocked that events had apparently taken such a rapid downturn that their leaders now felt the only appropriate action was to surrender.

Our Commandants around us are holding their own. Commandant Daly's splendid exploit in capturing Linenhall Barracks we all know. You must know also that the whole population, both clergy and laity, of this district are united in his praises. Commandant MacDonagh is established in an impregnable position reaching from the walls of Dublin Castle to Redmond's Hill and from Bishop Street to Stephen's Green.

(In Stephen's Green, Commandant – holds the College of Surgeons, one side of the square, a portion of the other side, and dominates the whole Green and all its entrances and exits.)

Commandant de Valera stretches in a position from the Gas Works to Westland Row, holding Boland's Bakery, Boland's Mills, Dublin South-Easter Railway Works, and dominating Merrion Square.

Commandant Kent holds the South Dublin Union and Guiness's Buildings to Marrowbone Lane, and controls James's Street and district. On two occassions the enemy effected a lodgment, and were driven out with great loss.

The men of North County Dublin are in the field, have occupied all the Police Barracks in the district, destroyed all the telegraph system on the Great Northern Railway up to Dundalk, and are operating against the trains of the Midland Great Western. Dundalk has sent 200 men to march upon Dublin, and in the other parts of the North our forces are

active and growing. In Galway Captain –, fresh after his escape from an Irish prison, is in the field with his men. Wexford and Wicklow are strong, and Cork and Kerry are equally acquitting themselves creditably. (We have every confidence that our Allies in Germany and kinsmen in America are straining every nerve to hasten matters on our behalf.)

As you know, I was wounded twice yesterday and am unable to move about, but have got my bed moved into the firing line, and with the assistance of your officers, will be just as useful to you as ever,

Courage, boys, we are winning, and in the hour of our victory let us not forget the splendid women who have everywhere stood by us and cheered us on. Never had men or woman a grander cause, never was a cause more grandly served.

(Signed). JAMES CONNOLLY,

Commandant-General, Dublin Division.

Arthur V. Matheson's Account of the Rising

The Easter Rising was predominantly a Dublin-centered rebellion which played out against the backdrop of Ireland's second most densely-populated city. As a result, while approximately only 1,600 Volunteers

A type of Armoured Car familiar in the Dublin Streets.

actively participated in the Rising, a large number of Dublin's 304,802 inhabitants found themselves caught up in the fighting. Some people, recognising the significance of what they were living through kept a record of what they observed and heard over the course of the week. Others aware that family and friends who lived elsewhere were concerned about their welfare, wrote to them, furnishing them with details of the Rising while offering reassurance that they were safe.

Arthur Victor Matheson, the Irish Free State's first Parliamentary Draftsman, responsible for drafting the 1937 Irish Constitution was one such character. In 1916 he was a 37 year old Dublin-born Barrister, who lived with his family at 20 Fitzwilliam Square, in the heart of Dublin city cente. On the 2nd May, he wrote to his sister Vera who lived in England with an account of his experiences and his thoughts

An Armoured Motor Wagon used in the revolt, built in eight hours in one of the Dublin Engieering Yards.

thoughts on the Rising. Arthur Matheson account is invaluable as it demonstrates how uninformed the vast majority of Dublin's inhabitants were of the Rising and its participants and how the Rising impacted ordinary citizens daily lives.

He begins his account by explaining that due to ill-health he have been in bed on Easter Monday and was unaware that anything was amiss until his father returned home from a walk in the city. His reference to 'the Sinn Féiners Volunteers' alludes to the fact that many ordinary citizens believed Arthur Griffith's political party was responsible for the rebellion. This belief would be maintained by some throughout 1916 and then following the amalgamation of Sinn Féin in 1917 with republicans and the formation of the new Sinn Féin party, it was accepted as fact. Matheson's suggestion that Francis Sheehy-Skeffington commanded the Volunteers in the Green is wholly inaccurate, but once again it underlies the limited information available to ordinary Dublin citizens.. The reality of course, was that Sheehy-Skeffington a committed pacifist, actively campaigned prior to his arrest for an end to the fighting. The numbers of casulaties was also greatly exaggerated but it demonstrates the genuine fear that existed among citizens for their personal safety.

I was not well at Easter and spent Easter Saturday in bed. I should have stayed in bed on Sunday also but did not, the result being that I had to stay in bed on Easter Monday, - during that Monday morning we heard a lot of shooting but

The ruins of Messrs. Eason & Sons' Premises, in Mid. Abbey St.

Inspection of Motor Ambulances at the Royal Barracks. May 27th

did not know what it was until Father went for a stroll in the afternoon and came back and told us that the Sinn Fein Volunteers had risen and seized Stephen's Green, the General Post Office and several other buildings. Their operations commenced about midday and were entirely unopposed. The Police withdrew to barracks as they were powerless against the Sinn Feiners who were armed with modern rifles. The Sinn Feiners in the Green were under the command of Sheehy-Skeffington and Countess Markowitz, the latter was marching about in male clothes and was seen shooting at some officers in khaki who were peacefully walking about the streets and also a number of civilians both men and women. They probably killed about fifty soldiers that way and anything up to a hundred civilians. The shooting civilians was a great mistake on their part as it turned the popular feeling against them. The Sinn Feiners stopped all trams and motor cars and made barricades in various places with them. They stopped a lot of motors returning from Fairyhouse Races. There was a good deal of casual firing on Monday night. On Tuesday morning the position was that the Sinn Feiners held Stephen's Green, The College of Surgeons and several other buildings round the Green.

The military were in the Shelbourne Hotel and the United Service Club (beside Robert Smyth's the grocers) and were firing on the Sinn Feiners in the Green. The military also had the Castle, T.C.D. and the Town Hall and all their own barracks but nothing else. The Sinn Feiners had all the Railway Stations, The G.P.O and several other buildings and shops, the Four Courts and Jacob's Biscuit Factory and Boland's Bakery at Ringsend. There was some looting on Monday night but not much. On Tuesday the provision shops were open and it was quite possible to walk about the streets and I believe there were crowds everywhere, walking and talking quietly and peaceably but feeling was strong and unanimous against Sinn Feiners. There were no soldiers or police in the streets. The Proclamation declaring martial Law came out about twelve o'clock (Tuesday). There were however, no letters, no newspapers and no telephones.

Like most Dublin citizens, the Matheson family continued to try and live their lives as normally as possible during the week's fighting. But Matheson's account of going to market on Wednesday morning illustrates the relative danger all inhabitants risked as they went about their daily lives.

About twelve Kathleen and I went to Harcourt Street to find out if the Clarkes had returned from Galway, we went by Adelaide Road and heard a lot of fighting going on round Portobello Barracks. We found the Clarkes had not returned (and they have not done so yet). The fighting then appeared to be getting brisk at the bottom of Harcourt Street (at the Stephens Green end) and also to be coming down from Portobello Barracks. Kathleen got a bit frightened and no wonder as there was a lot of shooting and noise which sounded very close. So we went down Hatch Street and so home without adventure, except that there were several shots, which appeared to be within a few yards of us. That was our last excursion except to market in the mornings. Kathleen fortunately got a good fright which has restrained her curiosity and personally I can control my curiosity very easily when there are bullets flying around. Father however, goes out exploring constantly and there are crowds in the streets watching the fighting as if it was a football march, several have been injured as a consequence and the wonder is that more have not been killed.

Our position here so far has been very curious and I hope it may continue so; I am touching wood while I write. There is heavy fighting all round us, in the Green, in the Portobello-Harcourt Road area and in the area between Haddington Road, Northumberland Road and the Canal. But so far no fighting and no troops have come near us. The Square is quite quiet, people strolling about and chatting, the weather is gloriously fine and all the time within half mile all round there is almost continuous firing, rifles, machine guns and some artillery.

There has been heavy fighting on Wednesday and Thursday on the bit of Northumberland Road between Haddington Road and the Canal and a good deal of casualties and all the time a large crowd on Baggot Street Bridge watching it. Last night (Thursday-Friday) there was heavy fighting in the City and a huge fire, so far as we can ascertain Sackville Street has been burnt down from Clery's to O'Connell Bridge on that (Clery's)

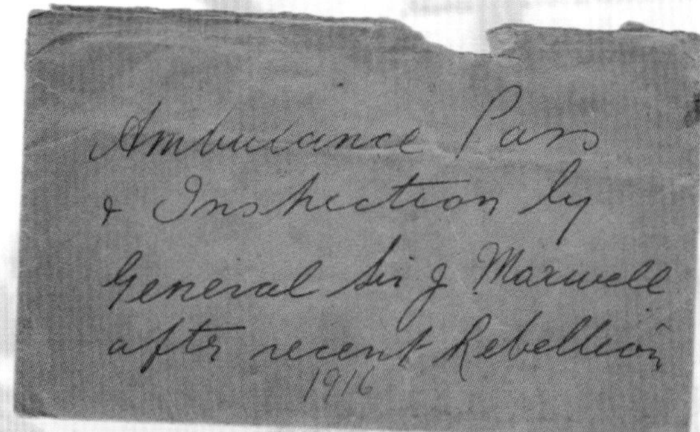

General Sir John Maxwell has a few words for each of the drivers & orderlies.

One of the two military prisonors held in the GPO, who were later rescued from the ruins of the Coliseum Theatre to where they had escaped.

side. How much has been burnt on the other side is not known, practically every shop in the city has been looted, until last night there were no soldiers in the streets except a few places where there was actual fighting and of course no police, so the scum of the city were free to do their worst. Fortunately, they did not come in to this district.

(N.B a bullet whizzed across in front of this (my study window) a moment ago, not close).

Our position at present is that we have had no letters or newspapers since Monday. Somebody in Fitzwilliam Place has a Daily Mail of today, and that is the first news we have got of what has happened out of Dublin and of course we ourselves only have second or third hand information as to what is in the aforesaid Daily Mail. Our provision shops have got no new supplies since Monday and are now sold out. We have only a little over twenty four hours food in the house.

By Friday the 29th, Matheson had gained a better understanding of those involved in the Rising and he tried to explain the intricacies of the Irish nationalist movement to his sister. Though the estimated number of Volunteers involved remains glaringly incorrect, it is interestingly that the Volunteer's association with Germany appears to be common knowledge.

There are supposed to be about 5000 or 6000 Sinn Feiners, all well-armed and with lots of ammunition and also supposed to be led by Germans. In case you do not understand who the Sinn Feiners are I should explain first that the Sinn Feiners are the Home Rulers who want complete separation from the British Empire, they are not Nationalists. The Nationalists only want a separate parliament - they want to remain in the British Empire. When the war broke out the Nationalist Volunteers split in two - one part followed Redmond and most of them enlisted - the other part followed a man called McNeill and remained more or less neutral, neither assisting nor opposing recruiting. The Sinn Fein Volunteers were an entirely different body, and was disloyal, and actively opposing recruiting. There was also a thing called the Citizens Army, which was composed of Larkin's followers and was disloyal and socialist. The men at present in Rebellion consist of the Sinn Fein Volunteers, the Citizens Army and some of the McNeill's Nationalist Volunteers. None of Redmond's Volunteers are involved at all. They are I believe, absolutely loyal and I think are actively assisting the military. At any rate they hate and disown the rebels. The rebels accordingly are not nationalists. They are a mixture of Socialists, anarchists, disloyal rebels and visionaries and fanatics. The wonder is that the rebellion did not fail through internal disputes - but in my opinion the rebels do not represent any section of Irish people or opinion except themselves.

The last Act - Prisoners being conveyed to the boats for deportation.

By Saturday, Matheson has grown increasingly concerned about the availability of food. It was a concern shared by many of Dublin's population as supplies were growing scarce. Aside from these domestic concerns, the sense seems to be that the general public have grown used to the fighting and are somewhat bored as a result of the implementation of Martial law and the military's curtailment of their movements.

During the past twenty four hours, our chief

Sisters of Charity feeding hungry boys during the revolt.

anxiety has been "food and how to obtain it". No bakers came round yesterday and we only got two loaves which father bought by a stroke of luck at Johnston Mooney and O'Brien's Bakery, Ballsbridge. I went out to said bakery before breakfast this morning but could get no bread. There was a crowd of about 200 people waiting at the bakery, but it was shut and no bread being sold. When Kathleen and I went out to market after breakfast we found a notice on Williams Shop that it would not open as all their supplies were sold out. We then went to McCarthy's, the Fruiterers opposite Irelands and bought some potatoes and apples which were all the vegetables they had. I saw a man carrying what looked like a parcel of flour with Ireland's name on it so I went across there and after some waiting got in and bought 1/4 stone of flour which was all they would give me. I also bought a couple of tins of corned beef to eat with the half ham Kathleen wisely bought a few days ago. Those purchases made rather a hole in a ten shilling note which was the only money any of us had. Things did not look very well accordingly just then but a short time afterwards Kathleen and Father discovered that the McConaghys (our butcher opposite Ireland's - we have left Cooney) had got leave to kill some cattle and had a shop full of meat. So they got enough meat to take us over Sunday and Monday which is a great relief as we had no meat. Father also got some money from McConaghy so are fairly alright for the present (touch wood).

A curious incident occurred this morning. Kathleen and I were looking out of my bedroom window about eight o'clock when we saw a party of about a dozen (estimates vary considerably)(somebody counted seventeen) Sinn Feiners ride up Upper Fitzwilliam Street on bicycles and go round the North and East side of the Square and disappear into Upper Pembroke Street. Most of them were in civilian clothes but all had rifles and bandoliers or bags of ammunition. There was nobody about except servant maids cleaning steps etc. Of course, there were no soldiers. Nothing further happened and nobody knows where the Sinn Feiners came from or where they went to, though it is generally believed that they are a party come up from Wicklow or Wexford to join the rebels in Dublin.

There was a lot of firing last night (Friday-Saturday) - rifles, machine guns, field artillery

Richmond Barracks used as a Detention Prison.

and what I believe is a naval gun. There was a big fire apparently near the top of Grafton Street and the fire in Sackville Street is still burning. We have no knowledge as to what is happening in regard the fighting - it is very difficult to locate the fighting by the noise alone. The military are not allowing any civilians near the fighting now and accordingly nobody knows anything but everybody has the most wonderful stories, all quite different and all mutually inconsistent. There are any amount of troops going into Dublin along Lower Mount Street and Merrion Square and a quantity of artillery went in by Upper Mount Street this morning. This is quite true because I have seen the troops from the street here with field glasses and Father and Kathleen saw the artillery.

We are getting pretty used to the firing now. Personally, it does not affect me at all and does not keep me awake but it is rather getting on Fathers nerves and both he and Kathleen still jump when they hear a shot closer than usual and it keeps them awake at night.

Once the mornings marketing is over, time hangs rather heavy on us as there is nothing to do or see and there is no use going out to the streets to talk to people as nobody has any reliable news.

We actually saw a newspaper today, it was not ours of course, but the owner very kindly stopped and let us read it. It was today's Daily Mail and cost the owner two-pence.

Writing on Monday 1st May, Matheson was aware the Rising had officially ended with the surrender of the Volunteers. Yet, he remains concerned that some rebels may be on the run and might still pose a threat. It is obvious from his remarks that while the Rising may have ended by the 1st May normal life for Dublin's inhabitants would not resume for some time.

Yesterday (Sunday) afternoon Father, Kathleen and I went in to town and Father met a solicitor who gave him a lot of reliable information. What we saw ourselves is, there are only a few bullet holes in the windows of the Shelbourne Hotel and the United Service Club. There are bullet marks all over the College of Surgeons and the windows thereof. Otherwise, there is no building damaged in Stephens Green. In Grafton Street, Noblett's, a sweet shop next

Noblett's, Leverets' and Fryers, Knowles, Woolworths and Mansfield's shoe shop have been looted and the fittings broken up. No other shop is looted or damaged in Grafton Street. There is no damage in Dame Street or any of the streets off it. Several shop windows are broken in Westmoreland Street but little or no looting. On the other side of the River, the position is very different. From Clery's to Hopkins every house is burnt to the ground except the front wall at Q.B.C is standing. Clery's and the Imperial Hotel are gutted, only the outside wall standing. From Hopkins along the Quays every house is burnt to about halfway to the Custom House. Liberty Hall appears to be in ruins but we could not see clearly. On the other side of Sackville Street, the G.P.O is burnt down, only the front wall and the pillars are left standing. Every house from Abbey Street to the G.P.O is burnt down including Mansfield's shoe shop, Easons and the whole of the Metropole Hotel. We are told a lot of Henry Street is burnt but we did not see it. Stephen's Green was locked but we could see the trenches dug at the four corners with rugs and cushions taken from motor cars still in them. We also saw in the trenches, two postmen's uniforms coats with the numbers and G.R badges etc. still on them. As the Sinn Feiners include a large number of minor Government officials, especially Post Office employees, the coats must have belonged to Sinn Feiners. We got rather a fright coming home up Leeson Street as there was shooting going on apparently in Hatch Street but we got home safely.

Nuns distributing food to the nesessitous poor.

From what the gentleman mentioned above told Father it appears that the position yesterday (Sunday) afternoon was that the College of Surgeons had surrendered and so had the Four Courts. Jacob's Factory had been evacuated by the Sinn Feiners and none of them had been captured but the soldiers got good hauls everywhere else - 70 at the Four Courts, and large numbers at the College of Surgeons and G.P.O - there was great slaughter of Sinn Feiners in Sackville Street, many being burnt in the fire.

Yesterday, (Sunday) morning there was heavy fighting apparently in Wilton Square and about seven there was much firing on Leeson Street Bridge. Things were fairly quiet last night, but this morning there was heavy firing on the far side of Merrion Square, which must have been either at Westland Row Station or Boland's Factory. We got ½ stone of flour today but no bread, meat or vegetables - we got only a small quantity of milk - we are however alright for the present as regards food.

We still have no letters, newspapers, trams, trains or telephones. The Police are about in plain clothes assisting the military and suspected houses are being visited and searched.

I have been going round the house and stables making all locks and bolts secure and am going now to fasten up the window opening on to the roof. We are afraid of wandering Sinn Feiners trying to get in to the house at night for food or shelter.

I hear the postal arrangements will be working tomorrow so I will close the "letter".

Your loving brother

Arthur

This letter was donated for use by Marie Keaney (nee) Carroll, family heirs of Arthur Matheson and Elliot. We the publishers are delighted to include exracts of this letter.

This book was compiled by Dr. Leanne Blaney.

Dr. Leanne Blaney recently completed her PhD in UCD's School of History. A former Irish Research Council Postgraduate Scholar, she has written extensively for various publications including the Irish Independent. Her main research interest lies in Irish social and cultural history in the nineteenth and twentieth centuries, particularly the history of transport.

Further Reading

Joost Augusteijn, *Patrick Pearse, The Making of a Revolutionary* (Basingstoke, 2010)

Joseph Brady, *Dublin Through Space and Time* (Dublin, 2001)

Joseph Brady, *Dublin 1930-1950: The Emergence of the Modern City* (Dublin, 2014)

Max Caulfield, *The Easter Rebellion* (Dublin, 1995)

Kathleen Clarke, *Revolutionary Woman: Kathleen Clarke, 1878-1972: An Autobiography* (Dublin, 1991)

Lorcan Collins, *16 Lives: James Connolly* (Dublin, 2012)

R.V. Comerford, *Ireland* (London, 2010)

Brian Crowley, *Patrick Pearse: A Life in Pictures* (Cork, 2013)

Mary E. Daly and Margaret O'Callaghan (Eds), *1916 in 1966: Commemorating the Easter Rising* (Dublin, 2007)

Paul Daly, *Creating Ireland, The Words and Events That Shaped Us* (Dublin, 2008)

C. Desmond Greeves, *The Life and Times of James Connolly* (London, 1961)

Ruth Dudley Edwards, *James Connolly* (Dublin, 1981)

Ruth Dudley Edwards, *Patrick Pearse: The Triumph of Failure* (London, 1990)

Seán Enright, *Easter Rising 1916 The Trials* (Kildare, 2014)

Ronan Fanning, *Fatal Path: British Government and Irish revolution 1910-1922* (London, 2013)

Brian Feeney, *16 Lives: Seán MacDiarmada* (Dublin, 2014)

Diarmaid Ferriter, *What If? Alternative Views of Twentieth-Century Ireland* (Dublin, 2006)

Diarmaid Ferriter, *Judging Dev* (Dublin, 2007)

Diarmaid Ferriter, *A Nation And Not A Rabble* (London, 2015)

Diarmaid Ferriter and Susannah Riordan (Eds.) *Years of Turbulence: The Irish Revolution and its Aftermath* (Dublin, 2015)

David Fitzpatrick, *Politics and Irish Life 1913-1921* (Cork, 1998)

R.F. Foster, *Vivid Face - The Revolutionary Generation in Ireland, 1890-1923*, (London, 2014)

Stephen Ferguson, *GPO Staff in 1916: Business as Usual* (Cork, 2012)

Richard B. Finnegan and Edward T. McCarron, *Ireland: Historical Echoes, Contemporary Politics* (Oxfrd, 2000)

Michael Foy & Brian Barton, *The Easter Rising* (Gloucestershire, 2004)

Mary Gallagher, *16 Lives: Éamonn Ceannt* (Dublin, 2014)

Roisín Higgins and Regina Uí Chollatáin, *The Life and After-Life of P.H. Pearse* (Dublin, 2009)

Roisín Higgins, *Transforming 1916: Meaning, Memory and The Fiftieth Anniversary of the Easter Rising* (Cork, 2012)

Brian Hughes, *16 Lives: Michael Mallin* (Dublin, 2012)

Shane Kenna, *16 Lives: Thomas MacDonagh* (Dublin, 2014)

Jim Keenan, *Dublin Cinemas: A Pictorial Selection* (Dublin, 2005)

Michael Laffan, *The Partition of Ireland 1911-1925* (Dublin, 1987)

Michael Laffan, *The Resurrection of Ireland: The Sinn Féin party, 1916-1923* (Cambridge, 1999)

Helen Litton, *16 Lives: Edward Daly* (Dublin, 2014)

Lucy MacDiarmaid, *At Home in the Revolution: What women said and did in 1916* (Dublin, 2015)

Breandán Mac Giolla Choille (Ed.) *Intelligence Notes 1913-16* (Dublin, 1966)

Ann Matthews, *Renegades: Irish Republican Women, 1900-1922* (Dublin, 2010)

Fearghal McGarry, *The Rising: Ireland: Easter 1916* (Oxford, 2010)

James McGuire and James Quinn (Eds), *Dictionary of Irish Biography: From the Earliest Times To The Year 2002* (Cambridge, 2009)

Donal Nevin, *James Connolly: 'A Full Life'* (Dublin, 2005)

Johann A. Norstedt, *Thomas MacDonagh: A Critical Biography* (Michigan, 1980)

Honor Ó Brolcháin, *16 Lives: Joseph Plunkett* (Dublin, 2012)

R. Rees, *Ireland 1905-25, Volume I Text & Historiography* (Newtownards, 1998)

Annie Ryan, *Witnesses: Inside the Easter Rising* (Dublin, 2005)

Charles Townsend, *Easter 1916: The Irish Rebellion* (London, 2005)

Clair Willis, *Dublin 1916: The Siege Of The GPO* (London, 2009)

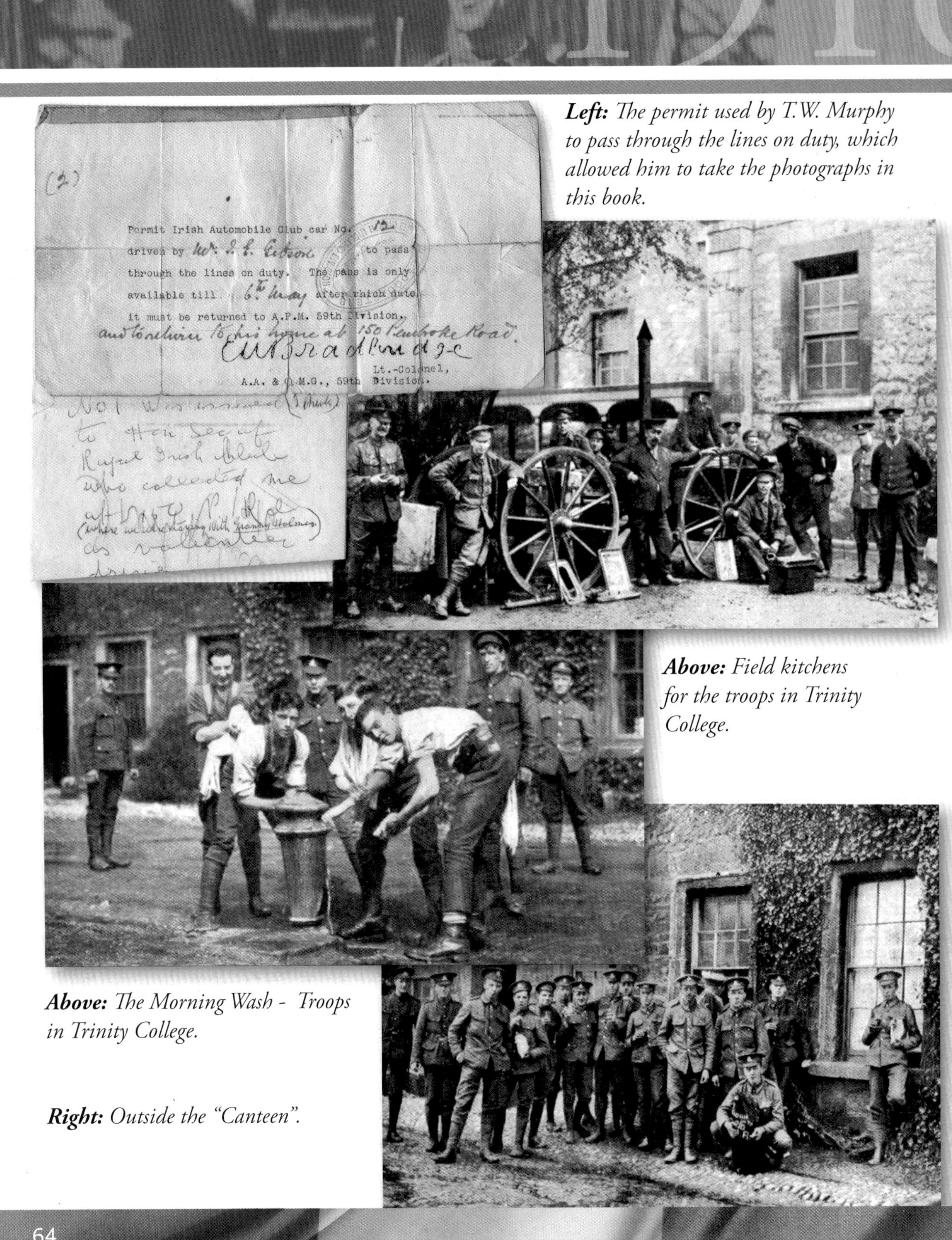

(2)

Permit Irish Automobile Club car No. 12
driven by Mr. J. E. Gibson to pass
through the lines on duty. The pass is only
available till 6th May after which date
it must be returned to A.P.M. 59th Division.
and to return to his home at 150 Pembroke Road.

E W Bradbridge
Lt.-Colonel,
A.A. & Q.M.G., 59th Division.

No 1 was issued (I think)
to Hon Sec of
Royal Irish Club
who collected me
at 150 P. Rd
(where we were staying with Granny Holmes)
as volunteer
driver

Left: *The permit used by T.W. Murphy to pass through the lines on duty, which allowed him to take the photographs in this book.*

Above: *Field kitchens for the troops in Trinity College.*

Above: *The Morning Wash - Troops in Trinity College.*

Right: *Outside the "Canteen".*